BLACK, MIXED WITH

Thank you for your support. With gratitude,

Grace Kuo

BLACK, MIXED WITH

Finding Authenticity through Adversity

ERICA KIDDER

NEW DEGREE PRESS
COPYRIGHT © 2021 ERICA KIDDER
All rights reserved.

BLACK, MIXED WITH
Finding Authenticity through Adversity

ISBN
978-1-63730-681-9   *Paperback*
978-1-63730-770-0   *Kindle Ebook*
979-8-88504-036-5   *Digital Ebook*

For my girls, Ava and Lena.

Your free spirit, genuine compassion, curiosity, and innocent wisdom inspire me every day. May you always embrace all that you are and live in your own authentic superpower.

You are my world.

CONTENTS

AUTHOR'S NOTE — 9
INTRODUCTION — 13

CHAPTER 1. RESILIENCE — 21
CHAPTER 2. BELONGING — 31
CHAPTER 3. ACCEPTANCE — 45
CHAPTER 4. FORGIVENESS — 55
CHAPTER 5. HOPE — 65
CHAPTER 6. INTENTION — 77
CHAPTER 7. JOY — 85
CHAPTER 8. COURAGE — 95
EPILOGUE — 103

ACKNOWLEDGMENTS — 109
APPENDIX — 115

AUTHOR'S NOTE

Thank you so much for reading *Black, Mixed With*. This book was born from the idea that embracing individuality, experience, perspective, and voice is at the heart of human connection. As a nation, what we have seen unfold in recent years has caused a divide on issues that are critical to the well-being of everyone. On the heels of the murder of George Floyd and Breonna Taylor, as well as countless other acts of racism and terrorism committed against Black and Brown communities across America, amid a global pandemic, economic uncertainty, and our arrival at the brink of what I see as a movement of inclusivity and equity, we need to raise up and be led by people of true and genuine hearts.

As I began to study leadership development, I started thinking deeply about authenticity and what that meant for me. During this work, I unpacked a unique paradox around identifying as multiracial. More specifically as "Black, mixed with." Amid my personal reckoning, I also wondered deeply about what authenticity means for you, what challenges and experiences you may be facing, and how you might be struggling with showing up as your authentic self in a world that often tries to predetermine individual acceptance.

As a child and a young adult, I always felt slightly out of place. And while I had many experiences that I point to throughout this book, at the time I couldn't quite figure out what it was that always made me feel like I was "other." What I have realized is that there was a constant internal contention connecting to identity markers that are culturally conflicting. Often, living in this intersectionality between two worlds led me to feel like I was not enough as I am, suppressing my voice and oftentimes feeling isolated.

As an adult, I noticed how systemic oppression, discrimination, and stereotypes led to misconceptions about my character. I felt the need to conform to societal standards and camouflage my true self as a survival mechanism. While I often felt that this was specific to me, I've learned that this wasn't just happening to me. My conversations and connections with others alongside countless hours of research have shown that living within diverse intersectionality can be a challenging experience. Black and Brown people are deeply affected physically, emotionally, and financially from the deep cuts of racism that have been seamlessly woven into the fabric of our nation. Women are reeling from sexism, struggling with pay inequities, harassment, and gender bias. As a result, no longer willing to remain silent, people are challenging the status quo, questioning norms and standards, and have raged a war on cultural intolerance. What we need now is a safe place to be where we can thrive while living our truth. *Black, Mixed With* is a celebration of who we truly are and the unalienable right we have to live freely, purposefully, and joyfully in all that we are.

My mission is to share inspiring stories, relatable for those of us who feel like we don't always belong. I want to demonstrate how you can break free from conventional thoughts and perspectives, ultimately embracing yourself for who you are. I want you to be empowered in your uniqueness, and I want you and the world to know that this is your superpower. You were not born to blend in—you were born to stand out.

INTRODUCTION

Catherine Wilbon, my grandmother, is my guardian angel and was my soul sister. We were born on the same day and share the same spirit. Catherine had the grace of Lena Horne, the genuine softness and wisdom of Mother Teresa, and as a former student at the Fashion Institute for Technology, she had the classic, vintage Jackie O. style. She traveled the world with my grandfather while he served in the military. During their fifty-three years together and the unconditional love for each other and their family, they experienced the pain of discrimination living in the segregated south, marched the civil rights movement of the 1960s, overcame traumatic systemic oppression, never wavering in their strength, hope, and faith. Passing these lessons on and speaking her words of wisdom, she would remind me to never let anyone or anything define me. You can overcome any obstacle, and in every challenge there is a lesson. Every experience is a gem—learn, grow, and transcend.

Fast forward a few years from when I sought the comfort of my grandma's house and the loving hugs I found there. I felt like a failure. I was working, looking for any opportunities to advance my education and obtain a higher pay, but I was broke. I ended my relationship with my daughter's father. I was on my own, building a life with a small child and balancing my life as single mother—and I'm Black. Even though I'm "mixed," I'm Black. I say that pointedly, because being African American, Brown, and/or Hispanic Latino is a specific experience particularly in relation to racism and systemic oppression. A 2014 article in the *New York Times* discusses the concept of new world slavery and describes it as stigmatization of skin color or the notion that a particular skin color signals one's status as a human being. Perpetuating this stigma implied that this treatment was both appropriate and necessary for the stigmatized. The concept of race itself is a construct that sends dehumanizing messages about some while elevating amplifying messages about others. As an adult, it became clear to me that there are challenges not only to living authentically having a Black experience but also to being "mixed" and in enduring stigmatized challenges that are often stereotyped and criticized (Jeffries, 2014).

While I was incredibly close to my grandmother, my family is pretty tight-knit for the most part. Like a mosaic, my family is very blended. They are a beautiful tapestry of diverse ethnic and cultural backgrounds. For the purposes of getting the lay of the land, I will tell you that my biological mother is Italian and Puerto Rican, and my biological father is Black. My stepmother is biracial or "Black, mixed with" like me, and my stepfather is Italian. This is the only time you will hear me delineate the titles of my parents. In my world, I have four parents and three brothers. My husband is White and my girls are multiracial, like me. This only skims the surface of the diverse nationalities and ethnicities within our family.

My dad's family is originally from Bronwood, Georgia. Reminiscing on Bronwood is beautiful nostalgia; it reminds me of the sweet comfort of my grandparents. It is the quintessential Southern and Black experience. It's everything you feel when you hear that Ray Charles song "Georgia," because it's exactly the place he is talking about when he sings that song. My eyes well with tears when I hear that song. Its words and orchestra are the "Georgia" I know and love. The road always leads back to that place.

My earliest memories in Georgia are of my grandparents, my cousins, and Big, my great-grandfather. Big's great-grandfather was a slave—imagine that. I knew my great-grandfather just like Big knew his, and his was a slave. Big lived through an era that we only read about, if we are fortunate enough to know the truth. Knight Riders lighting the sky with torches, burning down the Black-owned homes and Black churches. Jim Crow mandating segregation. Stories of undying faith and perseverance in the face of struggle. Those are the kinds of stories Big could tell.

I am the embodiment of generational poverty broken thanks to my mother's unwavering determination, courage, and bravery. My mom taught me how to be responsible, strong, and unwavering in the face of adversity, but still soft, kind, and sweet. No struggle exists that Liz couldn't overcome and not let that experience define her, break her, or make her someone that she is not. My mom and I got the grit and determination from my Grandma Lucy. A strong Italian woman, born and raised in Brooklyn, New York, she was a tough cookie. My Grandma was street-smart and could call you out on a dime. Fiercely independent, she marched to the beat of her own drum and lived her life the way that she wanted to: colorful and crazy. She was real, always herself, no matter what. If you knew her, you loved her for being who she was, unapologetically, all the time.

While my mom is half Italian, or half Italian and Greek as Ancestry.com hints, being Puerto Rican and owning Latino culture are a huge part of who I am. I'm a proud Puerto Rican like my Grandpa and my aunts and uncles. The only thing is, I don't speak Spanish fluently. No, I don't speak Spanish as a first language, I don't speak it fluently, and I would be lying if I said I spoke it well. I'll pause for the collective, "Que?" My grandfather speaks Spanish, my great grandmother only spoke Spanish, my aunts and uncles speak Spanish, my cousins speak Spanish, and my best friends speak Spanish. I try, I truly do. I took Spanish class from seventh grade to senior year. I bought books. I tried Rosetta Stone, Babel, virtual Spanish class as an adult, and only watching television in Spanish. I have watched one hundred and twenty episodes of Silvana Sin Lana and I still can't speak Spanish.

I share all of this with you because I think it's important to understand where people come from in understanding who they are. Who we are is uniquely imprinted by how we look, how we speak, and how we carry ourselves. I came to this realization while talking to a woman who has become a mentor to me. Also multiracial, her mother was from Costa Rica and her father was an Irish-American veteran. She said to me, "One day I was chatting with a gentleman and somehow it came out that my mother is from Costa Rica. He said to me, 'No way! Now I know what it is, now I know why I relate to you when you speak! You speak just like a Costa Rican, only you speak that way in English.'" This anecdote proves that we carry our culture with us everywhere we go. Every day you carry the mosaic of the cultures that make you up. For us, it may not be seen or heard, but it is most certainly felt.

For me, being "Black, mixed with" is having a marginalized experience in terms of experiencing racism, colorism, and oppression, all while having certain privileges. It means feeling isolated in "otherness" from lack of representation in places that validate my existence and visibility in the world.

"Black, mixed with" became the way in which I was most comfortable answering the common-to-me questions, "What are you?" and "Who am I?" We are all so many things. People are comprised of powerful virtues, strengths, gifts, and talents all together making up who they are. Culture and society have tried to classify that which is unclassifiable about many of us, and not fitting inside society's predefined box can be a lonely and challenging experience.

The response "Black, mixed with" was my answer and became a philosophy I embedded in my soul, the embodiment of who I am as a person. "Black, mixed with" is simply the realization that you and all of the beautiful virtues, strengths, talents, and gifts that make you whole are far more than the challenges that you have experienced, more than the labels that anyone has placed on you or the boxes of conformity that society has forced you into. Embracing authenticity is so important because it is the crux to seismic change. Being your authentic self gives others permission to be their authentic selves. Truly showing up as you becomes the pathway to human connection and the driver for purposeful change.

We all have strengths and talents that make us unique and diverse, but sometimes we hide what is true and beautiful about our nature to fit into what is perceived as "acceptable," essentially boxing us in and prohibiting free expression. Everyone has a thing, or a few things, that "hold them back," but where I think we get caught up is not recognizing the beauty in those challenges and embracing the lessons they have taught us. These are the situations that leave you at a crossroads, a turning point in your life. The events leading up to these situations are sometimes painful experiences or life's hard lessons, but they are the experiences that I am most thankful for.

Being transparent and authentic despite adversity is the catalyst for true change in leadership. Whether you are leading a Fortune 500 company, a team, or carpool of the future leaders of tomorrow, how you show up today exponentially shapes tomorrow. As a mother, a wife, and a warrior for change, I am proof that we do not and will not be defined by stigma, stereotype, or society. Throughout the book, I will share my stories, lessons, and takeaways to guide you in accepting what makes you different and celebrating your individuality.

We will uncover lessons and virtues in dealing with:
- How we remove the shame of challenging experiences and adversity and replace it with the courage to live truthfully, using it to build a bridge of empathy with others.
- The power of gratitude in transforming your mindset.
- How to harness the power of positive self-talk, self-belief, and manifestation
- How the alchemy of hope is the catalyst for transformation.

While my stories center around challenges with racism, colorism, sexism, and more, I share those because they are my experiences of intersectionality, but that doesn't limit the discussion. This is a celebration of diversity and what that means for you. This book is meant to inspire you to overcome challenges that hold you back to accept what makes you uniquely "you." My hope is that in reading this book you will discover that adversity is not shameful. Accepting and embracing challenges, regardless of what they are, cultivates your perspective. That diverse perspective is your best competitive advantage, your superpower. With these gifts that are uniquely yours, you are unstoppable.

CHAPTER 1

RESILIENCE

"I think there are three defining days in your life. Besides day one, when you are born, and the day when you discover your purpose, I believe there is a day in between. And that is the moment when you find out who you will not be, who you will not become."

—SUNNY HOSTIN

I was in survival mode. Let me tell you about survival mode: "Survival mode" is the physiological response your body has when you are under stress. These changes are basic to the human function of the body and have served us, our ancestors, and our cavemen ancestors since the beginning of mankind. You may know this as "fight or flight." Suppose you're sleeping, and in the middle of the night you hear a loud bang. You pop up out of a deep sleep with a quick burst of energy; that response is fight or flight. This is the body's stress response activated. Your body conjures up a concoction of hormones that gives you the energy you need to fight or flee from imminent danger.

Our body has this response to emotional stressors in our environment as well. For example, your body responds the same way regardless of whether there's a lion in the bush or the seventh bill collector calling. This is because we are unable to distinguish between actual threats and perceived threats, and as humans we react with the same physiological caveman response. While this phenomenon is incredibly useful, nature only intended it to be short term. After the threat has cleared, the body should return back to its normal state. However, prolonged physical and emotional stressors prevent that from happening, keeping people trapped in a prolonged fight-or-flight mode, therefore, stress is literally killing us. (Turmaud, 2020).

It's no secret. Health officials say that stress is a strong contributing factor to many health issues, both physically and mentally. The Mayo Clinic lists stress as a risk factor for heart disease and heart attacks, high blood pressure, weight gain, and digestive issues, just to name a few. Stress is a leading factor for patients with depression, anxiety, and other mental illnesses. While everyone has experienced stress in their life, their environment and experiences play a large part in what drives and triggers stress. The Minority Stress model explains that oppressed groups existing within social structures where there are greater incidents of prejudice and discrimination experience greater negative health impacts and disparities than those in the majority groups. I quote these statistics because they resonated with me. These were the odds for me, I was living proof of the data and the deck was stacked against me (Meyer, 2003).

I was living in survival mode, the stress was constant undercurrent and I knew at some point it was going to get the best of me. The pain and nauseous feeling of anxiety waved through my stomach as I maneuvered with precision around Government Center traffic in downtown Boston. Driving into Boston for work every day, I navigated with the kind of expertise that only comes from daily practice. I would drop my daughter off at daycare, and a frantic, oftentimes profanity-laced mad dash into the city would ensue. This is a tried-and-true test of heart health and driving capabilities.

Racing against the clock, I was always the last one in and the first one out. Praying that no one would notice I tried my best to live up to corporate expectations, but it was tough trying to stay a step ahead while always being a step behind, and a bill behind at that. Even though I was killing myself to portray an image of confidence and self-assurance at work, I was secretly tormented—emotionally tormented by phantoms. These phantoms stalked me throughout the years. They started as white noise, playing constantly in the background, and morphed into shadows of the subconscious. They attached themselves throughout the years as a consistent nagging, constantly reminding me that I am different and that I am other, pointing at incidents to prove to me that I was not worthy of true love or connection and that I was a failure.

It didn't take much for the phantoms to convince me that I was a failure: failing at work, failing at home, failing to be a good mother, and failing to follow my dreams and show up in the world as I really am. I swirled in a hurricane of shame for being who I was, feeling isolated in the shame, marginalization, and challenge of being a "Black, single mom."

I could tell you that a carton of milk costs three dollars and fifty-three cents. Sometimes that was all of the money I had.

I know all about overdraft fees, late fees, bank fees, and over-the-balance fees. I can dodge debt collectors with the best of the best and I can get you extra time to pay your electricity bill and keep the lights on, no candles required. I can tell you exactly how long it will take a check to clear if you sent it on Friday but are worried because your paycheck doesn't actually hit until the following Wednesday, and you really need to pay rent.

Every company was nice. People tended to be welcoming and friendly. No one was hateful in any sort of way but, just as it was when I was growing up, there would be ways in which I knew I was different. The office was usually predominantly White and predominantly male. Many of the people I worked with were highly educated. I often sat in a sea of Ivy League men in suits, most of them married with a few children, a dog, a white picket fence, or an ocean view. Often, they had very traditional families and traditional family views, a very different world from my world and the world that I grew up in. I couldn't help but feel out of place.

As much as I pondered our differences, I wondered if we were similar in any way. Did they secretly worry about their children while they were at work like I did? Were they ever worried that their children would notice how many hours they spent at work? Did they miss a first step or a basketball game? Were they as sick as I was over how many firsts they were missing out on?

As I navigated my way out of the city and into the suburbs, the rain began to pour. Oversized rain drops crashed on the windows like the knocks of a court gavel laying down the judgment: guilty. I was tired, tired of feeling like an outsider, like I could not and would not ever be able to be successful in this environment. I was tired of feeling like I had to wear a mask every day and hide my true self, putting on an act just to get through the day. I choked back tears for the ride back home. On these rides, I would often think to myself, "You've got this, what doesn't kill you makes you stronger," but I couldn't deny my intuitive response to that statement: "Yikes. That's bleak. So basically, what I am going through right now is the next best thing from death."

The storm raged on as I pulled into the daycare driveway. I made it with seven minutes to spare. Running back into the rain to the car, I pulled into my apartment complex already soaked from strapping Ava into the car seat. Wet, with my toddler hoisted on my hip, I pushed my way through the apartment doors into the musty smelling hallway, muscling my way down the hall and into my apartment with my three dollar-and-fifty-three cent milk in a bag and a thirty pound toddler on my hip.

My apartment was calm, like the calm after the storm, but it was haunted. The phantoms lived there as well. Ghosts of depression, anxiety, despair, and embarrassment skulked along the walls. These demons had become mine and they were unapologetic about their ridicule, gaslighting, and blaming as they followed me around. Constantly over my shoulder, they whispered strong rationales as to why all of my insecurities were true and accurate representations of who I was as a person.

"So pathetic," the Phantom whispered in my ear.

"Such an idiot," another confirmed.

Every night, I made Ava dinner but I didn't eat. Eating was lonely. Stress robbed me of an appetite. I was a skeleton for a frame, a shell of a person carried by ghosts of despair. Even though I didn't eat, I insisted that I make Ava dinner each night as a validation of good parenting and to make up for the guilt that I felt for working. In my mind, the least I could do was come home and make my child a decent meal.

Every night that I made dinner was a night that Ava didn't eat it, and tonight was no different. I broke up pieces of chicken and set them in front of Ava on a toddler tray. She immediately threw them on the floor, challenging me. Not willing to give up, I filled a spoon with little chopped carrots and went for the airplane in. With impeccable timing, my sweet baby girl knocked the spoon back at me, carrots flying in my face. I was stunned, hurt. Ava threw herself down in frustration, kicking and screaming with the vengeance only a toddler can have. I could hear the phantom taunting and jeering at my maternal heartache.

"See I told you she's a bad mom," ghosts snickered as they whisked by me.

I could feel the tears swell in my eyes. In an overflow of bottled emotion, I yelled at my baby, bursting into tears, "What the hell is wrong with you? Why won't you just eat?" I cried hard. I cried loud. My cry drowned the temper tantrum my daughter was throwing in tandem.

We cried a cry of utter frustration together. This was the figurative straw that broke the camel's back. My friend and I have coined this "dropping the ketchup." Dropping the ketchup is when your spouse does something (or many things) to annoy you and you don't say anything, keeping it bottled up until they accidentally drop the ketchup, something so small and so innocent. And you lose your ever-loving mind, threatening divorce over spilled Heinz, citing irreconcilable differences and obnoxious clumsiness in the courts as your reason for separation.

I dropped the proverbial ketchup on myself.

I was tired of being tired, tired of living in shame and embarrassment, tired of the constant anxiety, and tired of the feeling that I was in some way fundamentally flawed. I was a Black, broke, single mom. I was a statistic, and the numbers painted an even dimmer future. My dad always says, "The numbers don't lie."

According to data collected by the Statista Research Department there are over four million Black families with a single mother, which has increased from 1990 when it was reported that there were just over three million. While this data showed that the poverty rate declined among the Black and Latino populations, it also showed that the poverty gap is still disproportionate: Blacks and Latinos are still overrepresented in the population of poverty. For example, in the same data set Black Americans represented approximately thirteen percent of the total population but make up nearly twenty-four percent of the poverty population, proving that deep-rooted issues of systemic oppression continue to impact opportunities for education, employment, and work experience, which are critical elements to making not just a living wage but a life wage, and for the ability to build a future in which your children can thrive.

The waves of guilt and anxiety raced through my stomach again as I agonized over my consequences. I was guilty of creating generational patterns of disparity and I felt like I was facing a socioeconomic disparity life sentence for my daughter and me.

These feelings had been swelling for some time. The pressure mounting each day was driven by expectations—those I had for myself paired with those placed on Black and Brown women culturally. Our culture accepts and ingrains in us the expectation that women like me will always be single, Black, broke moms. After all, that is statistically accurate.

I knew this in my core. The example of this fate is too often depicted, sometimes the only depiction we see. The plight of the Black woman, many times is a box office hit. I was emotionally exhausted from the constant subconscious battle of proving my worth in ways that were more comfortable for other people. It's psychological warfare: constantly assessing and reassessing your environment to determine what the masses deem acceptable, and then contorting your identity to fit this predetermined mold for the sake of your survival and your personal safety.

On the floor next to my baby, I felt worthless, shameful, embarrassed, and not worthy of anyone's love, not even my own. When I looked up, my wide-eyed, tiny tyrant had snapped out of her little fit and was looking at me with her giraffe pacifier hanging from her mouth, watching me, studying me, and looking for an example as to what to do next. I had to get up and get my act together. While I may have been down and out, I still had a flicker of faith and my grandmother's encouraging words, her gems. I had the undeniable qualities passed down to me from my Mosaic: my mother's endurance, my dad's coaching, my grandma Lucy's toughness and grit and my uncle's entrepreneurial spirit. I knew that I had to stop being someone I was not, even if it felt a little out of place at times. In that moment, I knew exactly who I would not become.

I knew exactly who I was, and I had to give myself the permission to be myself because I was enough. I had everything I needed to overcome this. I could be more than this. Change starts in me, after all. I wiped my tears and said to myself: "I am enough, I am enough, I am enough," repeatedly and unapologetically. The phantoms slithered out of the room.

UNCUT GEMS
- Beyond the physical toll of elongated stressful periods, stress induces and perpetuates a fixed mindset, limiting focus and potential.
- Experiences do not define you—rather they shape your perspective, build character, and cultivate resiliency.
- You are enough.

CHAPTER 2

BELONGING

―

"You cannot define the undefinable."

—ERICA KIDDER

The first few weeks of high school for me felt like a rush; everything was new. I had never gone to a new school before. There were four schools in town and they all included a middle school, so I went to the same school from the time I was in kindergarten until eighth grade—same school, same kids, same teachers. Since there was only one high school in town, everyone who had previously attended one of the primary schools to complete elementary and middle school converged together at high school unless you went to private school.

I don't know if there were other multiracial kids at the other schools or not, but one thing was certain: there was mass confusion about what race I am. I realized quickly that I had to figure out how I was going to identify, because it was also clear to me that as the weeks went on, people were naturally gravitating toward the kids that looked like them. I started to notice that they would all go together. The Black kids hung out with the Black kids, the Latino kids hung out with the Latino kids, the White girls had a few different social circles and the White boys seemed to divide themselves by high school sports team affiliation. This is a huge generalization, but for the most part, that was how it went. Meanwhile, I was in between worlds.

I remember the day that I learned I was in between worlds and that I always would be. We were all gathered in the hallway of the school and there was always this chaotic flurry while changing classes. We were gossiping about some drama—we were about fourteen, so whatever the drama was I don't quite remember, but it involved another girl named Erica—and my friends were quick to clear up that it wasn't about me. No, it was the other Erica; not the Erica that talks like she's White, the other one.

"Am I the Erica that talks like she's White?" I asked.

My friends were quick to defend me again. "Don't worry, we told them that you just talk like that, but you're cool, though."

"Thanks, guys."

Besides people getting comfortable with the whole "talking like you're White thing," I noticed that people were more comfortable if they could racially classify me. Within the first few weeks of school I found an impressive list of identification classifications. I tried biracial; Mom is White, Dad is Black. Someone noted that meant I was "mulatto." In the noise and chaos of school, I thought they said I was *Milano* and I was excited. I had a word

I could use that someone had actually heard of before. I could make being *Milano* a thing. About two weeks later, I was sitting in history class and I learned what the term *mulatto* meant. I also realized that they were calling me *mulatto*, not *Milano*.

The term *mulatto* refers to someone with one Black parent and one White parent. Mixed-race individuals were commonly described as *mulatto* during the period of slavery in the United States. Okay, so they were somewhat right—not totally, but somewhat. This term, however, is from the Spanish root word *mulato*, which means "of mixed breed," and literally means "young mule," from *mulo*, or "mule"—and it's offensive. (*Merriam-Webster's Online Dictionary*, 2021)

After the *Milano* incident, I decided that I would just say, "I'm multiracial." Multiracial seemed to cover it, with the term *multi* meaning more than two, but I felt like it was lacking one major point about my identity: I am Black. Being Black is just as much a part of the experience as being "mixed."

Even though high school was the first time I had to problem solve my race, it wasn't the first time I experienced the confusion or the need for comfort around racial classification. The issue always crept up, especially when filling out forms: "Please choose one." This was a common theme that went as far back as elementary school.

I sat at my desk, waiting as the teacher passed out the test book packets to each student. The classroom bustled with the regular activity of a classroom full of sixth graders. The desks were arranged in typical rows facing the board. The boys were in the back making typical boy ruckus. I sat at my desk next to my best friend, and as usual we chatted away. This day was a fairly typical school day, except that we were staying in homeroom for most of the day because we were required to complete a portion of the state-required standardized testing. I believe in schools today this is all entirely computerized, but in the 1990s that was not the case, so the teacher distributed those thinner-than-paper, flimsy paper books with the waxy coating that are not quite gray, not quite white, and never quite soaked up the pencil so it always left pencil lead residue on the side of your hand.

The teacher made several attempts to quiet the class. She distributed the booklets to each student one by one, going over the instructions multiple times in what I found to be annoying detail. She repeated the instructions louder in another attempt to quiet the class.

You know, if they miss the instructions because they are talking, too bad for them. I can read, and you don't have to shout, I thought to myself.

Sometimes I found it annoying that the boys in the back were always catered to even when they were misbehaving. I followed along with the teacher reading the instructions again. With each page flip, the paper made a distinct little crackle. I read on.

In the boxes below, please fill in the circle for your ethnicity (please choose one).

I studied the question. *How do I select one? What if you are not just one? Should I say I'm Black? No, I can't just write*

Black—*aren't I also what my mom is? Maybe I should write Hispanic.* I read and reread it again. *The answer reads Hispanic Non-Caucasian, but I am Hispanic and Caucasian. I think Italian is Caucasian. I can't write Caucasian because that says Caucasian Non-Hispanic, and I am Caucasian* and *Hispanic* and *Black. What an oxymoron this is!* I made the following selections:
1. Black/African American
2. Caucasian (*Non Hispanic*)
3. Hispanic *(Non Caucasian)*
4. Other *(Please Specify):* American

I was satisfied with my answer, but I didn't like the question and I didn't like that I was being forced to choose. I definitely didn't want to tell a half-truth. I figured whoever was reading it would understand. They had to get it, right? They probably see this all the time. Used to not having the best answer for those types of questions, I moved on to the remaining exam questions. By the time I had completed the test, I had forgotten all about the question—until about an hour after we submitted the books.

We moved on to the last period of the day and I was sitting at the lab tables in science class chatting away with my best friend. In the middle of my story, I was interrupted by the guidance counselor standing in the doorway.

"Erica, please," she said, elbows crossed, wearing her annoyance on her face.

I looked up, confused. *Me?* I thought. *Why does she want me? It's usually Jacob or Billy she calls for when they hide stink bombs, or like the time that Tyler G. put a dead frog from the science lab in the cafeteria salad—that was disgusting. I think that was the only time I actually heard of someone being expelled from school. Either way, those are always the kids that get dragged down to guidance or the principal, not me.*

I never got in trouble. I avoided trouble like the plague. I made sure I was well liked and on my best behavior. The principal would pass me in the hallway and call me "Erica Willy Wilbon," pinching my cheeks and telling me, "You're such a good kid," and I liked to keep it that way. My dad always said, "You have two things in your world: your good name and your good credit." I didn't have credit and I wasn't quite sure what that was, but I had a name and I tried to keep it in good standing.

Something must have happened; the counselor looked disappointed in me, not concerned for me. I slowly got up, totally aware that the whole class was staring at me, wondering the same thing: What did she do?

A couple of the boys heckled me from the back of the classroom, saying, "Uh-oh . . . what'd you do? Willy's in trouble."

"Oh, big trouble," another echoed.

Their taunting made the walk of shame from desk to door even more embarrassing. I walked with my head down. *Don't make eye contact,* I thought. I exited the room and walked down the hall, butterflies dancing in my stomach as I ran through a list of potential reasons why I could be in trouble in my head.

Okay, Erica, think . . . think . . . what'd you do? Had I said something fresh to one of the teacher aids at recess? Did someone tell on me for something? I wondered if I'd gotten a bad grade. I wondered if they realized I am really bad at math. I wondered if they were going to send me to one of those special classes because my math was so bad I couldn't even pass the sixth grade. By the time we reached the office, I was in full freak-out mode—silently, in my head of course.

The guidance counselor sat down in her chair. I sat down as well. She slid the test booklet in front of me from across the table.

"Do you think this is funny?" she asked me, very directly, very sternly. Clearly, she thought that I believed I was being silly or cute on an official state test.

"No," I replied.

"Then why did you mark all of them when you were only supposed to pick one, and then write in 'American?' You were trying to be funny with that."

Yes, she was right. I was being snarky because I was annoyed by the question and being forced to choose. But I am American, and I was still satisfied with my answer and with going against the written rule because there was no right answer to choose.

"I didn't know what to write down." I said, head down, feeling the weight of her judgment.

"Why don't you just write Black? You are Black aren't you?"

"My dad is Black."

"So there you go, Erica, erase those and fill in the circle for Black."

"But I'm not just Black. My Mom is Puerto Rican."

"Then check the box for Hispanic," she said.

"But that box says Hispanic Non-Caucasian, and my mom is White."

"You just said that your mom is Hispanic."

"She is, but she's Italian also."

I could see the guidance counselor becoming increasingly more frustrated with my answer.

"Honestly, Erica, you're Black. Just check the box for Black."

I checked her box and walked out of the office.

Up until recently, people who are biracial, multiracial or "Black, mixed with" represented less than three percent of the population on paper, but likely have always been a larger part of the population with no accurate way to identify, existing only in the shadows and shrouded under a history of shame. Biracial babies started as the children of slave masters and their slaves. Laws were subsequently put into place to make interracial relationships—and thus, our existence—illegal.

Additionally, laws such as the "one-drop rule" meant that you could identify as Black only if you were one-fifth or even one-drop Black.

After 1967 interracial marriages were legal in all fifty states. After marrying in Washington DC, seventeen-year-old Mildred Jeter (who was Black) and her childhood sweetheart, twenty-three-year-old Richard Loving, returned to Virginia to visit family. They were arrested and charged with unlawful cohabitation under the state of Virginia's miscegenation laws which banned marriage between Blacks and Whites. After a landmark case in the United States Supreme court, *Loving v. Virginia* (1967), the Supreme Court ruled that state bans on interracial marriage were unconstitutional. The date of the ruling, June 12th, 1967, is now known as Loving Day and is celebrated by many to honor our freedom to love and marry whom we choose. (ACLU, 2021)

While legal to exist since 1967, census boxes remained an issue until the year 2000 when it became legal to self-identify as biracial/multiracial on the national census. As reported by Faye Fiore for the LA Times in 1997, the Clinton administration adopted recommendations made unanimously by a thirty-agency task force assembled to address the concerns of multiracial Americans, many of whom were upset at the government's attempt to wedge them into a rigid category by insisting that they identify themselves as members of a single race. As such, the government adopted new questions on the United States Census forms which allowed for the selection of "multiracial" and the ability to identify with more than one race. As Sally Katzen, an OMB administrator, said, "public participation is particularly important because it reminds us constantly that there are people behind the numbers and for many, this is a deeply personal issue." White officials had to acknowledge this.

The boxes are a big deal. Some of the comments I have received when I've mentioned this are cavalier, like I was making a big deal out of something that maybe wasn't actually a big deal. I thought that might be the case until recently. I came across an article on NPR released in 2013 on the same topic. Dave Kung, a half-White and half-Chinese math professor, was in his late twenties when his 2000 census form arrived, offering him the chance to check more than one race box. Kung said that "when I filled out my census card and was finally allowed to correctly check more than one box, I cried."

My parents didn't teach me color or show me boxes—the world did. Color was not a thing in our house. How could it be? We all loved each other, and my parents provided a loving and nurturing home. I never distinguished a color or assigned any attributes to the people I entrusted with my survival. The difference in shade never crossed my mind. We all walked around with color-blind filters on. There is no judgment on the face of those who love and care for you. The color or age or gender of the hands that respond to your every need hold no significance. I never saw color until the world taught me how to see color to determine where I belong and with whom I would be accepted.

At this point, I would be remiss to not discuss the other elements at play. While racism is high on the list of challenges as identifying as "Black, mixed with," there is another contender: colorism. Colorism has as long a history in this country as slavery and has been carried on throughout generations in many different examples.

During the 1920s, jazz music was just taking off. Going out to the jazz clubs was all the rage. The Brown Paper Bag Test was coined in the 1920s during this era. One of the most renown jazz clubs was in Harlem, and it was called the Cotton Club. Along with their musicians the club was also known for its dancers, the Copper-Colored Gals, a dance troop of light-skinned dancers. The rule was that to be a dancer you couldn't be a shade darker than a brown paper bag. That term is still used today to describe your proximity to Whiteness and privilege (Mernin, 2016). Examples of this have been seen over the past decades and have been recorded widely in educational institutions and universities, churches, and social clubs. People describe denied entrance, affiliation, or participation within the Black community (Ferris State University, 2013).

I became keenly aware of colorism in college. Within the first weeks of being there, I had quickly gained a few enemies. I didn't quite understand the looks or the attitude, but this group of girls was immediately off-putting, immediately rude, and immediately aggressive. After each run in with them on campus I would wonder what I did or where we got off on the wrong foot. One day in Spanish class the girls were sitting in the row that I generally sat in. The seat I usually occupied was free, so I asked if I could slide down that row. I knew it was going to be a problem, but I also thought that I would show them I wasn't scared of them, and I had no idea what their problem was.

They both stood up to let me and then the girl closest to me hip checked me into the seat. I fell into the chair, shocked. The girls laughed and the whole room looked.

"Oops, looks like you fell!" they said, laughing.

"My bad, my bad," one girl said, laughing so hard you would think she might fall out of her chair. The class laughed right along with them, thinking that I tripped and fell.

My insides were burning.

"I didn't fall!" I told my friends, fired up after I left class. "Those basketball [feel free to insert a profane noun here], hip checked me into the seat!" I was with my friend Annie, who I met that year at college, and her friend, O. O was mixed like me. O could have passed for my sister.

"I don't know what I did to them. We've barely been on campus a month and I have never had one positive interaction with them, and I don't even know them, couldn't even tell you their names. I don't know what I did to be literally physically assaulted."

O looked me dead in the eye and said, "Girl, we are light and they hate us because of it. That's why you got hip checked."

Perhaps I was naïve, but the thought had never crossed my mind. I was shocked that O thought so, because up until this point I thought we were Black like them.

I reconciled this confusion all the time. I had experienced the embarrassment and isolation of racism. I knew I wasn't White and being no stranger to racial slurs in school, I was sure not to forget it. Racially motivated microaggressions stayed with me from the first one ever uttered. From the boys in class calling me a monkey to being referred to as "nappy-headed child," their words constantly played in the background of my mind like the white noise of ghosts, taunting me. Keenly aware I didn't fit in there, I felt uncomfortable identifying as "Latina," though I feel strongly that I am Latina.

My family is proud to be Puerto Rican, so I naturally felt that I identified as Puerto Rican as well. However, a strong value of identifying as Puerto Rican is that many Latinos speak Spanish as a first language or fluently, as it's the only language spoken at home. I didn't. My mom is Latina but doesn't speak Spanish, so naturally the only Spanish I speak is the Spanish I have learned on my own. That made me feel like I was the furthest thing from being a Latina, and based on my experience in college, it is not safe to say that I can fully identify as Black either.

I am an occupant of a world that is in the middle. My time in the middle has taught me something very valuable: the element of inexactness is universal and innate to all of us, but there is risk to your sense of belonging and your authenticity in this place. We hide or camouflage parts of ourselves to blend in because we fear that we will not be accepted or belong. Belonging becomes the sacrifice of authenticity.

The world goes out of its way to classify the unclassifiable. If we think about who we are versus what the world wants us to be, we are all an anomaly. Honesty, transparency, and vulnerability are what allow us to understand others, connect to others, and build a bridge of empathy. Human connection is fundamental to our existence. Like a human race common denominator, it is the most common thread among us. In recent years, we have seen continuous attempts to push division among people—be it racial and ethnic, gender-based, political, or religious—but marching alongside are rising movements joining forces to unite humanity.

UNCUT GEMS
- Inexactness is innate to all of us.
- Belonging should not be at the sacrifice of authenticity. People need to be able to feel like they belong and have the freedom to be their true self and embrace the power authenticity brings.
- The belonging that matters is the sense of belonging that we feel when connected to ourselves, the sense that we deeply know and embrace ourselves.

CHAPTER 3

ACCEPTANCE

---

*"Even if it makes everyone uncomfortable,
I will love who I am."*

—JANELLE MONÁE

My hair was the first indicator to me that I was different. It's as "mixed" as I am. I joke that my hair is like the United Nations: Italy on the top, Spain and Portugal at the bottom and sides, and Nigeria in the middle. My youngest daughter has the same unique pattern (you're welcome, Beanie). My hair is fine, but there is a lot of it. A mix of wool and cotton, my afro is all coils and curls and a patch of kinky in the middle. Frizzy and not porous, my hair is dry and brittle. As a kid, I had trouble maintaining my hair, so it didn't grow well and was always breaking. No one around me had any idea how to deal with my mane.

The feeling of being different and trying to meet the beauty mark struck me in kindergarten. I distinctly remember the feeling of the first day of school excitement. Do you remember that? Everything felt new, like turning over a new leaf. What would your teacher be like? What new friends would you meet? Which old friends would you see? Would this be the year I make straight A's or try out for the talent show? The beginning of the new school year always felt like endless possibilities to me, but in the middle of that excitement I felt different from the other girls in my class.

I knew that I looked a little bit different from them, but what stood out to me was how different my hair was from the other girls'. At a very early age, I recognized the contrast and felt that their hair more closely resembled how pretty hair should look. I remember the way they flipped their hair to the side or tucked a piece behind their ear. Their hair was always long, shiny, straight, and glossy—exactly like the models on TV or like the pretty actresses I aspired to be. The girls in my class would swing their hair like you see in those Pantene commercials. Light reflected off their strands. Their hair had elasticity. To me, they looked perfect, and I longed to be perfect like them.

I feel like it always smelled great too, flowery and fruity like in that Herbal Essence commercial. My hair never smelled like fruit and flowers—it smelled more like earthy oils and the scent of our pink lotion and Blue Magic hair grease. I really wanted that hair swing and shine, but beads and braids don't float softly through the air. The fact of the matter was I didn't have access to hair care education. At that time, my options for Black hair care products included Black Magic hair grease, Pink Lotion, and Just for Me relaxers. No internet, Pinterest, TikTok tutorial, or YouTube influencer could show me how this whole mixed-girl-hair thing worked.

Growing up, my hair struggle plagued me. I think that everyone struggles with something. Everyone has something about their experience that they are not comfortable with. For some, it could be weight, a language barrier, gender identification, or uncovering or sharing a disability. No one's genetic makeup is exactly the same, nor is the human condition experienced by each individual. Every one of us will experience life and life's challenges in a different way.

When you're faced with a challenge to your fundamental existence, regardless of what it may be, you go through survival mode and develop a skill set to survive. For me, I needed a suit of armor. I needed to be more inconspicuous, more . . . ambiguous.

On that topic, queue the second week of sophomore year.

"Oh my God, girl!" I proclaimed as my high school friend came strutting through English class looking like Christina Aguilera. (Side bar, in the early 2000s, you weren't true friends if you didn't call each other "girl.")

She was my English class buddy, a mutual friend of a friend. She was blonde, usually with medium-ish length hair, longer than her chin but shorter than her shoulder. This day though, she had eighteen inches of blonde, luxurious mermaid hair, and I was absolutely blown away by this sorcery.

"Girl, where did this hair come from and how do I get it?"

My friend explained the magic on her mane was called hair extensions. She bought extensions of human or human-like hair and sewed them into a braid of her own hair, and voila! She added an additional twelve inches to the length of her hair and a volume rivaling that of Diana Ross, all for one hundred and sixty-five dollars.

My new goal was to get this hair. For six weeks, I did extra chores, babysat, bussed tables, and scrounged couch cushions for change. I came up with exactly one hundred and sixty-five dollars. (No tip—sorry about that.) I grabbed my money and begged my parents for a ride to the salon.

Four hours later and a twirl in the mirror, I was hooked. I strutted out of there with a cute half-up, half-down look of straight, shiny hairstyle. It blew in the wind. It smelled good. I finally felt like I was pretty. My hair was long, straight, and glossy, pretty by everyone's standards now.

That summer, I strutted my hair extensions to southwest Georgia. Every other summer or so my family took a twenty-two-hour drive—yes, twenty-two hours exactly, I counted them—down to Albany, Georgia for a family reunion. My favorite memories of visiting my cousins were spending time with the family, making up dance routines with my cousins, getting ready for church, and going to church.

Getting together with my cousins was always an explosion of stories and expressive dramatizations. My cousins were always curious about my very northeast Boston accent. Even in my best attempt, it's hard to hide the stereotypical "pahk the cah in havahd yahd," no Rs annunciated. My cousins couldn't hide their urban country twang.

I arrived at my aunt's house, fresh off my twenty-two-hour drive, and almost immediately my cousins were all about what was going on with my hair.

"Oh, this?" I said innocently, trying to play it off like it was no big deal. "It's just some hair extensions."

"Hair extensions? Girl, that's a weave and it needs help!"

"A weave?"

"Yes, boo, a weave! You have a weave. Look at the back!" My cousin turned me around. "You see how they weaved them tracks into... well, I guess they're supposed to be cornrows back there... but yes, ma'am, you have a weave and we need to fix it."

I dropped my head and reached in for her hands to feel the braids in the back of my head. *A weave?* I pondered. I had never even heard that term before. My cousins agreed to do my hair, so we headed to the hair store. I had never been.

When we parked, I was astonished! I had died and gone to hair heaven. I must have looked like a kid at Disney or like the tourists in New York, the ones that just stand there staring at the beautiful chaos of the city. In southwest Georgia, they had a whole store dedicated to hair. Black hair care products, weaves, wigs, brushes, blow dryers, hot combs, flat irons, all on displays from wall to wall. This store was dedicated to the perfection of Black hair. This was my Mecca.

Here's the thing: hair stores and braiding existed where I lived. They just weren't around me. This was the first time I saw girls who looked like me, felt like me, and did something about it. They made it work for them in brown, black, Lil' Kim blonde, Yaki straight, curly, wet-to-dry, natural and synthetic—all ranging from ten to twenty-six inches. For about a hundred dollars, you could look like you hit the genetic gene pool. Feeling lousy about yourself? Grab a pack or two of Brazilian hair and run your fingers through the bundle, and feel your soul instantly lifted out of the gutter. There were moisturizers, oils, conditioners, gels, and creams for all different patterns and textures of hair. This began my era of hair exploration. I found the armor I needed.

Along with a weave, I've done the big chop. The big chop is when you cut off damaged or chemically processed hair, opting to wear shorter, natural hair. My big chop grew out into an asymmetrical bob. The asymmetry was not intentional even though I tried to play it off like I was doing something trendy. The reality was that one side of my hair didn't grow as fast, broke off, or was damaged. I know a stylist is going to want to fight me after that statement, but regardless of how it happened it was shorter than the other side, so asymmetry and hoop earnings were a thing for roughly eight days.

I perfected the wash-n-go, roller sets, twist-outs, braids, braid-out, relaxers, also known as "creamy crack" thanks to the Chris Rock documentary, *Good Hair*, got off the creamy crack, back to natural, silk press, and Brazilian blow outs *(Stilson, 2009)*. But no matter what I did, I still felt off, uncomfortable, and insecure. Long, shiny, and straight still had my heart.

Between our culture and the media, the concept of Whiteness as the acceptable beauty standard has been intentionally and seamlessly programmed into our society as a mark of colonization. Extending beyond the States, this is a globally recognized and felt phenomenon that has bred White supremacy into the undercurrents of our culture. As a direct challenge to the notion of what it means to be beautiful, entire movements have united as a force to expand our idea of beautiful to be a more inclusive and accurate representation of the diversity of all people.

Alongside the Civil Rights movement formed the "Black is Beautiful" movement of the 1960s and 70s, affirming beauty and embracing the political power of beauty in Blackness, which was previously considered ugly or undesirable. The indigenismo movement was a driving force along the same lines. Popularized by Frida Kahlo, who painted herself in native clothes with facial hair, fueling an artistic form of the radical rejection of Eurocentric beauty standards. More and more, we are seeing the unity of people standing together in body positivity and humanity-based movements to embrace the dismantling of the beauty system and representation systems that enable continued oppression. We are embracing unconditional self-love and acceptance in all aspects of who we are (Donnella, 2019).

While we have taken steps to broaden the definition of beauty, this concept still has a chokehold on generations of people. I've talked to countless Black and Brown women and have learned that self-image, representation, and self-esteem are all challenges on the journey of self-acceptance. While doing research for this book, I spoke to a girl named Annie. Annie is fifteen, thoughtful, and honest. Annie is "Black, mixed with," like me. She has a fresh perspective and an old soul. She's as real as they come, wearing a vintage Pearl Jam t-shirt and an Afro that rivals Angela Davis'. I realize that times have changed since I was fifteen, and I wanted to know what it was like for Annie identifying as biracial in today's world.

One of the key differences I learned from my conversation with Annie is that some things have changed and some things have not. I mentioned before that I believe we are on an inclusivity and equity movement. You may say this is because our communities are much more diverse now. To that, I would say yes and no. Yes, the gaps are shrinking, but I actually think one of the main driving factors for the uptick in diversity is because people are more comfortable publicly identifying and there are more ways to do so. We are fixing the literal box-checking issue, but unfortunately, the other familiar elements are still there. Isolation, the mass confusion of racial inexactness, and the frustration of a lack of representation lurk around Annie, too.

"Erica, I started to realize that even if I straighten my hair, I'm still not going to look like them. I really looked in the mirror and thought, *I will never look like them because I look Black.* I have Black features. My nose is wide. They don't have this nose. These lines when you smile, what is that? I will always look different no matter what, and even though they put Black girls on TV, they still don't look like me. They might be Brown or Black, but they never have a wide nose or the smile-line thing. They still always have a small, pointed nose and straight hair; they still look White."

Adequate representation is critical because it affects the way people see you and treat you. If you are represented in the media, you are represented in the world. That visual representation of you is equally as beautiful as all other represented people. Representation means that your existence is acknowledged and accepted. More important than being represented and accepted in the media is accepting ourselves. It starts with self-acceptance, loving yourself, and showing your true self to the world.

I didn't realize that my hair acceptance journey was really a journey of self-acceptance. Like a chameleon shedding layers of its skin, I continually grew and moved toward not just acceptance but authenticity for myself. What I learned is that no matter what your hairstyle, wardrobe, or bank account looks like, you will not be happy if you don't love yourself. Regardless of representation, stereotype, popular opinion, or any other reason, I had to accept and love myself. No matter what anyone else said or what anyone else thought, I had to shamelessly own everything about myself: skin, hair, Black, single, broke—all of it.

The challenges, the triumphs, the failed attempts—all of it made up the experience that shaped my perspective, and my perspective is valuable. These lived experiences contextualize and nuance behavior, thinking, and judgment. When I accepted what I believed was flawed about myself, my challenges became a connection point, an allyship, and a shared understanding instead of a stigma, judgment, or criticism. Everyone has a challenge, something about their experience that makes them unique and different, something that has shaped their unique perspective.

My hair was the first step toward reimagining and rewording the narrative around the parts of my experience that I found shameful. Was I a single mother with an abhorrent list of reasons why I should carry so much guilt and shame, or was I unbelievably fortunate to be someone's mother and to get to stand up and be the role model and example she needs me to be? What good can come from this experience? What gift, curated in these experiences, can I offer the world? I can offer the challenge to live beyond the shame, to find self-love and acceptance in all that we are on this journey. Hair love was the beginning of my self-love.

UNCUT GEMS
- Self-acceptance builds a connection point to others so there is space for an allyship and a bridge for shared understanding.
- Representation means that your existence is acknowledged and accepted but more importantly than being represented and accepted in the media, we need to accept ourselves.
- The wins, losses, challenges, triumphs, and failed attempts comprise the experience that shapes perspective. Dimensions of perspective are the core of diversity, and uniqueness in experience is universal to everyone.

CHAPTER 4

FORGIVENESS

—

"You have the power to envision a better world. Be brave enough to look into the face of great challenges and let the truth of the struggles you see inspire you to imagine your way out, knowing all the while that your individual imagining is also a social imagining."

—TERERAI TRENT

I have a confession. I can be a bit of a grudge holder. I know it's petty. I know no one is perfect. Forgiveness is a virtue that I must work on. Then comes the hurt. The hurt is in the memory. The cycle continues.

I sat in a hotel room in northern New Hampshire on a weekend getaway trip with my husband and daughter. We were excited to take Ava up there, and we planned on going to a few amusement parks in the area. But in this moment, Colby and I were glued to the television in our hotel room.

We watched as a group of White nationalists clashed with a group of protesters denouncing racism on the streets of Charlottesville, Virginia, during what the local paper called the "Unite the Right Rally." The event estimated that approximately two thousand to six thousand people were expected to attend and sought to unify the far-right wing and, according to the group's Facebook page, "affirm the right of the southerners and the people to organize for their interests." Witnesses reported to NBC that a car plowed into a group described as "anti-racist" demonstrators, killing a woman.

NBC reported that The King Center—founded by civil rights icon Martin Luther King Jr.'s widow, Coretta Scott King—had tweeted that "racism never left America." In this moment, I couldn't have agreed more (Mcauliffe, 2017).

It became very clear to me how wide the gap was. These men were terrified that the concept of equality would somehow marginalize them, as if asking for equality in systems of oppression would be replacing them, as if the concept of equality for both sides is mutually exclusive. They were angry, terrified, and irrational. We watched, horrified, as they rioted in fear of losing the legacy of White supremacy.

This fear is not the kind that makes you run screaming out of a room or jump out of your seat. It is more like an undercurrent of edginess, silent but always lurking around. It creeps up on you even in the mundane moments of everyday life, like working, driving, and walking about. Sometimes it creeps up as a reaction to microaggressions when you ask yourself, "Do they realize what they just said?" Sometimes it bubbles to the surface in response to obviously racist remarks and comments—"Did they really *mean* what they just said?" Other times it boils to the top like hot lava, like the paralyzing shock, disbelief, and undeniable sadness at the police brutality and killings against unarmed Black men, a confirmation of the Black community's distrust in law enforcement.

As the day rolled on and the coverage continued, so did the national conversation around race. After spending the day with Ava, we went back to our hotel and began to wind down for the night. The television was on, broadcasting coverage of the riot. Colby and I half listened to the news and half scrolled through our phones on social media as Ava slept comfortably on the pullout sofa next to the bed. Mindlessly scrolling, I began to focus on the argument going on between my members of my family.

Unfortunately, I have witnessed my family post pictures in honor of the Confederate flag, liken the acronym of Black Lives Matter (BLM) to "Burning, Looting and Murder," and comment that a Black politician should pull her big lips over her head as that may get her to shut up. The racist rhetoric they spewed in response to the Charlottesville riot was no different. They went on what had become their typical rant. As I scrolled, I saw comments likening Black Americans to animals and statements saying that "Black people should all go back to where we came from." As loud as those hateful comments were, the silence from others who I would have expected to speak out was deafening.

I never understood the term "seeing red" more clearly. I saw red, every shade of red—fire engine red, scarlet red, mahogany red, currant red, and blood red. Fire red energy blocked out anything else and anyone else in the room. I felt the energy of intense rage as I read the bigoted confirmations of betrayal.

Before this moment, when I thought about the concept of family, I thought about unconditional love, connection, and solidarity. After that moment, I could never look at these members of my family the same way again. Another reason this discovery was so striking to me is that my family is a military family. Everyone in my family knows each other from living in integrated neighborhoods and going to integrated schools on base.

This is not coincidental. In 1948, President Truman signed Executive Order 9981, ending the segregation of the US Armed Forces and repudiating one hundred and seventy years of sanctioned discrimination. While Truman previously held and spoke on his racist viewpoints, he was disturbed by the lynchings of Black soldiers who had returned home from fighting. In response to those killings Truman formed the President's Committee on Civil Rights, where they wrote *To Secure These Rights*, a report condemning segregation and asking for an immediate end to discrimination and segregation in the armed services. Within six years, all branches of the United States Army were desegregated, opening new pathways for African Americans to hold rank and positions.

On the fiftieth anniversary of the signing of the Executive Order, General Colin Powell said "the military was the only institution in all of America—because of Harry Truman—where a young Black kid, now twenty-one years old, could dream the dream he dared not think about at age eleven. It was the one place where the only thing that counted was courage, where the color of your guts and the color of your blood was more important than the color of your skin" (Evans, 2020).

My family is so integrated and served in not only an institution that pioneered integration but an institution that is called upon to protect the fundamental rights of this nation that was built on the backs of a melting pot of people in search of the "American Dream." The fact that they are so uncomfortable because of my mixed heritage race is unfathomable and contrary to the values of our constitution. It was shocking and hurtful that people I once believed would protect and love me are of the exact ideology that has not only caused so much hurt, suffering, pain, and detrimental divisiveness, but that threatens my well-being and the well-being of my father, my brothers, and people who look like us. I had full validation of what was true and the realization that I had been duped. Apparently, everything I felt growing up was a very logical response to the environment I had been in. It wasn't just in my head that I felt a distinct feeling of difference.

"People don't remember what you said, but they remember how it made them feel."
—MAYA ANGELOU (GALLO, 2014)

Ultimately, how you speak emulates how you think. How you think directly affects your actions. Therefore, hate speech and discriminatory language is perhaps the strongest catalyst for hateful actions and discrimination because it stems from a place of thought rooted deep in our psychology. This is incredibly dangerous to the livelihood of Black and Brown

Americans and is not something I am willing to tolerate in any capacity—family or otherwise.

When the initial rage subsided, I felt an overwhelming sense of grief. I grieved my family. I grieved the family I once had and the family that I knew now was gone. You love them unconditionally because you always felt you were a part of them, but then you realize that they never really felt the same way about you. That's where it hurts.

> "Darkness cannot drive out darkness; only light can do that. Hate cannot drive out hate; only love can do that."
> —MARTIN LUTHER KING, 1957 (DANIELS, 2021)

While I am a self-proclaimed grudge holder, what my experience has taught me is that there is peace in forgiveness and that there are boundaries in the breadth of forgiveness. Without forgiveness we operate from anger, and I don't think that anything can be solved operating from a place of anger. Colby says to me, "It's okay to be angry. Anger is a normal emotion." He's right. We are all human and can be angered, but what we have seen and what we can say that has not been successful is the dance of anger and forgiveness laced in trust. I trusted you, you wronged me. I am angry, so I wrong you. You are angry, so you wronged me. The cycle continues. Upon reflection on the comparison of anger versus forgiveness, I thought it would be natural that the opposite of anger would be forgiveness, but now I believe that forgiveness is the antidote for anger.

About a year later, the Black community grieved another murder of an unarmed Black man, Botham Jean. This time, the murder was committed by a White female police officer, Amber Guyger, who said that she mistook his apartment for hers after a long day at work. At Guyger's conviction hearing, where she was sentenced to murder in the first degree and ordered to serve ten years behind bars, Jean's brother gave an emotional speech in which he tells Guyger that he forgives her. At the end of his emotional speech, he asks the judge permission to hug Amber Guyger.

The gesture was met with controversy. Some called the ten-year sentence a "slap in the face." Others in the Black community fear that the willingness to forgive will perpetuate more violence against Black people. Brandt Jean defended his decision to hug his brother's killer at an acceptance speech after he was awarded the 2019 Ethical Courage Award from the Institute of Law Enforcement administration, saying, "After being found guilty by a jury of her peers, sentenced under the law, Ms. Guyger needed to be forgiven, and I needed to be free from the burden of unforgiveness." (NBC DFW, 2019)

Jean goes on to ask law enforcement officers in the room think to twice before taking deadly action. "I want you all to know that I am not a threat—that young Black males are not inherently dangerous or criminal. I implore you to champion the causes and procedures that amplify the value of all lives."

Regardless of how anyone felt about the hug, I did see the actions as demonstration of a path forward. Regarding the senseless killings of unarmed Black men in this country, I am not saying that the racial discrimination and violence in this country can be "hugged out."

What I am saying is that anger is catabolic energy and catabolic energy is not energy that results in movement forward, understanding, or true change. Catabolic energy is painful to the holder, not the receiver. Not forgiving is like drinking poison but expecting another person to die. Forgiveness is not about healing them, but about healing you.

What I have also learned is that forgiveness happens in your own time and is not necessarily reconciliation. For me, it is not. I will not reconcile with the likes of the ghosts of my past. The gaslighting ghost of not enough, the demon of blame and the phantoms of shame no longer harbor space in my heart, but it took a conscious effort to feel the warmth of the light where so much darkness had once lurked. Over time, I have consciously changed the energy in my spirit to release the anger that arises when I think of them, when I must interact with them, and when I recognize those demons haunting the shadows again.

I believe that forgiveness is not the absence of anger, pain, hurt, or sorrow, but the acknowledgment and conscious effort of releasing the visceral energy of those feelings from your body, refocusing that energy into a neutral energy—one less determinantal to your mental, emotional, and physical well-being. I am in no way saying that forgiveness and hugs are a resolution for the racism, discrimination, and violence experienced in this country. I do however feel that finding forgiveness and grace in your heart could be a chance at finding a path of healing moving forward in personal relationships, difficult discussions, uncomfortable conversations, and difficult things that ultimately help us grow.

UNCUT GEMS
- Forgiveness happens in your own time and is not synonymous with reconciliation.
- Without forgiveness, there is no possibility to collectively move forward.
- Forgiveness is the antidote to anger.

CHAPTER 5

HOPE

"There's something beautiful in being who you are and being comfortable with whatever your voice is."

—ANGIE MARTINEZ

Here's a thing I haven't mentioned: I love hip-hop. Hip-hop touches my soul and speaks to my spirit. It tells the truth and sparks drive, offering unwavering confidence, encouragement, and faith to me. Hip-hop is a first friend, coach, therapist, stylist, scholar, and philosopher. I am not alone in my hip-hop obsession; my dad loves Hip-hop as well, and as the adage goes, "the apple doesn't fall too far from the tree."

When I was growing up, my dad was a software engineer by day and a DJ by night. He would DJ clubs, birthday parties, bar mitzvahs, graduation parties, benefits, corporate parties—you name it, my dad had a few records to spin up and was a master on the turntables. Going through my dad's crates of records, I listened to artists like Sugar Hill Gang, Kurtis Blow, and Grandmaster Flash. Slick Rick the Ruler and

Dougie Fresh were family party favorites. My first cassette tape was TLC's *Ooooooohhh... On the TLC Tip*. T-Boz, Lisa Left (Left Eye) Lopes, and Chili made it cool to wear the street style that you felt most comfortable in and hang out with who you wanted, and preached authenticity, femininity, and girl power (TLC, 1992). My first CD was Kris Kross' album *Totally Krossed Out* (Dupri, 1992). Determined to stand out, every hip-hop artist had a unique style. Kriss Kross was no different with the backward jeans, a wild trend that swept the early part of the nineties, putting a nuance on the baggy style that would be signature to the decade. I got ready for school to De La Soul's "Me, Myself and I" off the album *3 Feet High and Rising*; and listened to A Tribe Called Quest's album *The Low End Theory*, on my Walkman on the way there. Their uplifting beats and confidence-building messages fueled my motivation throughout the morning *(De La Soul, 1989, A Tribe Called Quest, 1991)*.

Hip-hop is a history lesson of untold Black stories, stories about where we came from, our hope, determination, and faith as a people—faith to rise above marginalization. Hip-hop artists embrace the struggle, never letting the odds win, using the proverbial "rocks thrown" to build an empire. While hip-hop may get a bad reputation for having explicit and profane lyrics and content, regardless of the words used to express the story, the message of true hip-hop remains one of hope, justice, tenacity, grit, and the sheer ambition of an underdog. Hip-hop artists pride themselves on preaching self-love, intrinsic self-belief, unique style, and individualism, creating a culture built on the strength and unwavering hope of the Black and Brown urban community and telling a story of a human experience that may not have otherwise been heard.

Between 1968 and 1978, the politics and socioeconomics of New York City and its boroughs set the stage for turmoil, drugs, and despair in the poorest areas of the city, sparking one of the darkest eras in New York's history: the South Bronx fires. Even before the fires, banks began redlining the area of the South Bronx and other urban areas. Redlining is the practice by which cities and financial and insurance institutions would lay out maps and draw lines around neighborhoods, evaluating the financial risk of lending or insuring. Neighborhoods that were made up of more than five percent Black or Hispanic/Latino people were deemed "declining neighborhoods." This practice prohibited banks from lending mortgages and loans or being able to acquire homeowners or fire insurance in these neighborhoods.

After redlining, the state of New York implemented the Urban Renewal project. The Urban Renewal project was a city project which demolished the housing complexes of predominantly Black and Latino families to make way for more expensive housing. Coined the "Negro Removal Project" by James Baldwin—novelist, poet, and activist—Urban Renewal allowed for systemic demolition of homes and caused the displacement of hundreds of thousands of predominantly Black and Latino families, becoming a driving cause of homelessness, joblessness, and crime in the city boroughs. One area notoriously affected by this migration was the South Bronx (Vazquez, Hildebran, Irizarry, 2019).

As years passed, the city and the landlords neglected upkeep. As opposed to upkeep, the city cut funding and closed the fire departments to reduce cost for New York City, which was facing bankruptcy. Buildings decayed and property value plummeted. Getting creative, landlords found financial restitution in the State Insurance Pool, which insured otherwise uninsurable property: the redlined property of the South Bronx. Landlords and the financially desperate people in the community looked to the profits of arson. Records show that in 1974 the State Insurance Pool paid out ten million dollars, and by the end of 1980, the insurance company Lloyd's of London paid out forty-five million in arson insurance claims. Nowhere was it required that the landlords who received those funds reinvest them back into the building or the community. Landlords responsible for torching their buildings and blaming "arson" walked away with insurance money free and clear, while the neighborhoods of South Bronx and inner-city areas rotted, decayed, and declined, becoming almost unrecognizable from the prosperous places that they once were. The result, a massive uptick in crime, drugs, poverty, and gang violence that tore through the city, terrified the community and sensationalized Black crime in the media (Vazquez, Hildebran, Irizarry, 2019).

While it may have seemed that neglect and avoidance of people living in ruins and ash could silence a community, a phoenix of new sound rooted in innovation and resourcefulness arose and forever changed the course of music. Not only did it create an entirely new genre, hip-hop created a new way of life, a movement and culture that brought people together in community, creativity, and hope, shining a little bit of light and fun in a city in darkness. This new genre had a few telltale characteristics—a recipe, if you will, that helped accelerate hip-hop into greatness. While hip-hop is innovative and creative, the focus on self-expression and individuality was something required and never seen before on this scale. The hip-hop pioneers' guiding principles were based on individuality. Uniqueness in flow, tone, sound, overall look, signature, and authentic rhymes are the cornerstones of hip-hop culture.

Hip-hop has come a long way since flames lit the skies of the Bronx in the sixties and seventies. It has since sky-rocketed into an artistic art form of self-expression spanning generations generations and racial and gender divisions, proving itself to be a bridge from what was once a silenced community to what is now mainstream media. Now an art form, hip-hop scholars identified six artistic elements in hip-hop culture, including the artistic handling of beats, spoken word and poetry, dance, writing, theatre and literature, and the knowledge of self (The Kennedy Center, 2021).

Beyond art, hip-hop represents the soul of a community. Akin to church for some people, it reminds us that where we've been is no indication of where we are going. Hip-hop is the scripture for defying the odds when they're stacked against you, and for doing so with style and a little bit of swagger. An outlet of artistic expression of lyrical stories and creative storytelling in the urban, Black vernacular, hip-hop tells the story of what was seen and what was lived as Black and Brown Americans. Hip-hop songs are lyrical stories of systemic oppression, discrimination, marginalization, and ultimately, of overcoming what would have been, what was, and unfortunately what still is a dim fate for so many.

The parks and streets of New York came alive with the beat of a new decade: the eighties. Explosive in base and upbeat, onlookers of these legendary verse battles couldn't help but dance to the beat of this stylistic new genre. Break dancing or simply "breaking," as the artistic call it, is the co-creator of the hip-hop culture that swept the eighties. From complex pops, drops, and locks to body flips and leg twists, this high-energy dance birthed a whole new style, pairing alongside hip-hop's most explosive lyrics and beats and becoming one of the most symbolic dances of the decade. This whole new style of dance borrowed moves from the early twentieth century and loosely imitated entertainers like Charlie Chaplin with his infamous walk and ad-libs, James Brown with his energy, and Elvis Presley's provocative nature. These borrowed pieces all transformed into a unique, stylistic dance revolution that swept the eighties and changed the landscape of pop culture. The duo of hip-hop and breaking was forever cemented into American culture, signed, sealed, and delivered with a distinct autograph: graffiti. Artistic outlaws who prided themselves on not only being the most resourceful and creative, but outlaws of government and wanted by the city—the most fearless artists of their time—made city walls into canvases (The Kennedy Center, 2021).

Born out of crisis and turmoil and transcending into a cultural phenomenon, hip-hop has influenced and transformed from a small movement on the streets of New York to an entire globally-recognized culture. Describing rags to riches stories, hip-hop is built on messages of hope, endurance, passion, ambition, real grit, and determination, while being musically rooted in innovation, resourcefulness, creativity, spark, and fight. Hip-hop is about finding a light, that flicker of faith in the darkest moments and in life's hardest lessons. Now a platform for people no longer silenced, no longer hidden, no longer a stigma, and no longer shameful, hip-hop is a beautiful, creative, and authentic expression of the human experience. If transformation had a playlist, it would be comprised entirely of hip-hop music.

What I love most about hip-hop is the message of hope that it brings. C.R. Snyder—a psychologist who studied "positive psychology" and who is internationally known for his work on the Hope Model—theorizes that hope is not an emotion but rather a cognitive process that occurs as a result of setting goals, having the tenacity to pursue them, and having the belief in your abilities to be successful. If we go by Snyder's definition, then the alchemy of hope is the catalyst for transformation. By putting into action the cognitive disciplines of Snyder's Hope Model focused on strategies to achieve goals, intrinsic self-belief, and motivation we can develop, live from, and sustain a positive place of hope (Snyder, 2002).

My daughter Ava has to have everything defined. It's how she rolls. She needs a definition, a purpose, and a timeline for everything. At first, this quirk of exactness used to irritate me, but I learned that this was her way of making the intangible tangible, and it gave her the clarity to focus on the vision, the mission, or at least the task at hand. Most things we wrote down and defined for Ava had a better chance of being accomplished, compared to the items or tasks that we didn't jot down. This isn't a coincidence.

Dr. Gail Matthews, a psychology professor at the Dominican University in California, studied the art and science of goal setting and found that you are forty-two percent more likely to achieve your goals by consistently writing them down.

Her study consisted of two hundred and sixty-seven people. The group included men and women from all different parts of the world who worked in all different occupations. The results were clear: the likelihood of accomplishing your goals increases when you write your goals down. Invoking that same spirit, I began to write out my dreams. Write it out. Write out everything. Find your way to create a visual representation of what you want to accomplish. This gives you exactness and makes whatever your dreaming of accomplishing "a thing." Not to mention, we write down the things that are important to us (Morrissey, 2017).

While Ava needs the exactness that I don't always like to commit to, she and I have one thing in common: we are dreamers. As a dreamer, I have incredibly high standards for what I what to achieve. For some reason, my thought process does not seem to compute that all of these things take time and energy, and I cannot harness all of the world's energy to achieve them in one day. I often have to remind myself that my desire for achievement is a process, a journey that can be accomplished one day at a time by taking steps. It doesn't matter what size steps, small or large things that seem unattainable can be achieved by taking actionable steps. Without this reminder, we can fall into an overwhelming thought pattern which leads to exhaustion or procrastination.

I procrastinate the dream. I procrastinate the to-do because I am overwhelmed about the doing, and then I feel bad. This is a slippery slope. Trying to boil the ocean causes massive waves of anxiety, not to mention it can be downright scary, like standing on a ledge and wondering, "Will I fly, or will I fall?"

I was that person with my head in the clouds, daydreaming away and thinking of a master plan but not really executing it. The problem with always dreaming and not doing is that there is no change without action. Action is kinetic. Even a small amount of action has a snowball effect. "Rome wasn't built in one day" I know is so cliché, but it is true. This thing you're building is built brick by brick, just like you and curated by you. What steps do you need to get there? Maybe those steps are even too big to accomplish right this very second, so break it down even further. What's the next best small thing that you can do today to make progress on this goal? If it makes you feel a twinge nervous, not frightened but a little giddy, it's likely the right next step.

Another way to power your productivity and ignite your motivation is to focus your efforts on "your top three." In his best-selling book, *The Productivity Project*, Chris Bailey writes extensively about this technique. Bailey says that out of the thousands of productivity tactics he has experimented with, "the Rule of Three" has emerged as one of the absolute best ways to have a positive impact on productivity, noting that "having just three items to focus on will help you stay centered and accomplish more" (Bailey, 2016).

This is a great way to focus your energy on the goals to move your vision forward. The fuel to hope is your momentum and your magic, your inertia, and the proof that if you stay the course, you're sure to get to where you're going.

How you talk to yourself matters. This statement has been made time and time again. The best rappers all have the reputation of songs about their confidence, success, and belief in their own authenticity. From the Notorious B.I.G.'s "Juicy" to Kendrick Lamar's "Backseat Freestyle," the positive affirmation of hope, power, self-love, and confidence is unmatched—so much so that these artists, even own their flaws (Wallace, Mtume, 1994), (Lamar, Hollis, 2012).

I find that the top three thought patterns to change for the combination of growth and movement are around excuses and the stories we tell ourselves: stories of why we can't, why we shouldn't, or why we don't deserve success or growth. Pay attention to how you talk to yourself and redirect or rephrase limiting thought patterns and beliefs. Some people write positive notes to say to themselves on little sticky notes and post them on mirrors and computer screens; I listen to Drake.

The real spark in changing the way you talk to yourself is in shifting your mindset. The book *Mindset: The New Psychology for Success* describes two aspects on an individual's mindset: the fixed mindset and the growth mindset. A fixed mindset is having a set of beliefs that limits achievement. These thoughts turn allies into critics, lead to inferior learning strategies, and limit potential. A growth mindset is the opposite. In a growth mindset, it would be almost inconceivable that a challenge could not be overcome or a goal not reached. This research shows that while some mindsets may be acquired in different ways, such as inherited or generational beliefs or results of environmental and social conditioning, mindsets can be changed. Your beliefs are a choice (Dweck, 2016).

According to Dweck, the limiting mindset is carrying shame and stigma. Dweck says, "Is there something in your past that you think measured you? Put that in a growth mindset, look at it honestly and look at your role and understand that it doesn't decide your intellect or your personality. Instead ask, what did I or what can I learn from that experience? How can I use that as a basis for growth? Carry that with you instead."

I fundamentally believe that the key to change is in your mindset. My dad used to tell me all the time, "Whether you think you can or you think you can't, either way, you are right." Or he would say, "The real four-letter word is *can't*." Dad jokes they may be, but he is right. Your beliefs drive your thoughts. Thoughts drive your behavior; therefore your belief system, the story that you are telling yourself, the script you are both writing and reading from, is the one dictating the outcomes. Take inventory on the story you have been telling yourself about you. Whatever that message is, remember that you are going around each day seeking validation of that message.

We can be incredibly hard on ourselves. I am definitely my own worst critic. The trick to true change is to ditch your inner critic and focus only on positive thoughts, positive self-talk, and positive inner monologues. Visualize where you want to go, see your dream in vivid detail, and believe that you, as you are, can achieve it. See it, say it, believe it, and no matter what, write it down. You can write positive sticky notes all over to remind yourself or listen to Drake—whatever helps you believe it with your whole heart.

UNCUT GEMS
- The alchemy of hope is the catalyst for transformation.
- If you want to make progress on something write it down. What we write down has more of a chance of getting done.
- How you talk to yourself matters. Your beliefs are a choice, so choose wisely.

CHAPTER 6

INTENTION

"See yourself as the creator of your own destiny—knowing that you have the power to shape your future and achieve your dreams.

—TERERAI TRENT

I dream a lot and I dream big. I love to share my dreams with the people I am close to. My dreams are my sanctuary, a place of immeasurable possibility. I am the dweller of my dreams and the keeper of my highest visions. I can't help it—I think big all the time. Even though in early 2013 it seemed like every dream was out of reach, I was still talking about them. During a trip with my one of friends, we spent four hours or the better part of the entire car ride from New York to Boston talking and envisioning the life of our dreams. At some point during the car ride, we started talking about our life, our future, what we wanted, what we didn't want, and what we were no longer willing to put up with in relationships, friendships, family, and work. We talked about what we would compromise on and the vision that we had for ourselves. Reviewing approximately a decade of lessons learned the hard way made parts of the conversation heartbreaking, but it was honest, riveting, and at times pretty hilarious.

We went on for hours laughing, crying, defining, and verbalizing the life we dreamed of. We didn't think anything of it at the time. When we talk about that day now, we both consider that day to be a turning point in the trajectory of our lives. This day was day one of intentionally building the life we dreamed of. Intentionality changed my world.

"Intentional living means understanding your fundamental beliefs and values, and then actively living your life in line with those values" (Stanton, 2021). Intentionality looks different to everyone; each person is different, as are their beliefs, values, and purpose. For me, intentionality means thoughts control actions. To set intention is to put energy toward what is important to you, on purpose. Sometimes, our thoughts can be reactive. We can get to a place where we live our life on autopilot in comparison to others, not being true to who we really are and what would truly bring us joy (Montague, 2020).

Setting intentions for your life can manifest in a number of ways. Whether the intention is big or small, it's been my experience that living with intention can shape your life. Einstein observed, "Nothing changes until something moves." That something is you. And the movement you need is intention. Intention enables you to live with heart rather than habit (Thackray, 2017).

After the car ride, I began to set my intention and my focus on my values and living authentically through what was most important to me. As a single mother, I had held high standards for my circle, especially those in my inner circle who would be around my daughter. An ambitious dreamer, I knew that I would only seek the partnership of someone who was supportive. As a somewhat wounded empath, I knew that I needed someone with the same ability I have to see the good in others, and to see and honor the good in me.

I met Colby on Halloween of 2015. Ava was terrified of Halloween and was scared for her life to go trick or treating, so I was fortunate to be able to find kid coverage to go out on a date that night feeling somewhat mom-guilt free. I told a wee lie—I know, the authenticity author told a lie . . . yep! I led him to believe that I lived about forty-five miles closer than I did in reality. We met online and I was a little bit wary about giving a "stranger"—by stranger I mean someone I had no prior knowledge of and had never met in person—all of my coordinates. I did not lie about what was most critical—my core values, my belief system, and who I truly was. It mattered to me that he knew from the beginning that I am a mother and we are a package deal. I want to share a life with someone, and someday I want marriage. I am family-centric, honest, loyal, a free spirit, colorful, crazy, determined, strong-willed, quick-tempered, and easily calmed, but most importantly I am worthy. And I want to build a life with someone who knows that they are, too.

I never knew my husband the day before I met him, and I know it sounds cliché, but when I met him I had known him for a hundred years. His essence, who he is, is exactly what I dreamed and everything I asked for. I had spent so long seeing the good in everyone and everything; my husband sees the good in me because I was able to show him the best of me through the intentionality of knowing what was important to me and focusing on serving that.

From acceptance rose the concept of worthiness. Worthiness drives intentionality. From the belief that you are worthy is the action to achieve that of which you are worthy. Intentionality and manifestation are pseudoscientific ideas, but ultimately it is the idea that your thoughts and beliefs can become real, and that setting your intention each day is the catalyst to the manifestation of your dreams. Understanding and accepting who you are, embracing your worthiness, and knowing your values are key to unlocking your dreams. This is how you begin to live intentionally. I believe that living intentionally in who you truly are is the key to dream manifestation.

Intentionality starts with acceptance. Only in acceptance could I truly believe that I was worthy of what I dreamed. When you know your worth, it becomes incomprehensible to settle for less than what you truly want. I believe that intentionality is the most radical form of self-acceptance. Intentionality is the tinder to the fire; intuition is the spark to the flame.

Intuition is the natural ability or power that makes it possible to know something without any proof or evidence: a feeling that guides a person to act a certain way without fully understanding why *(Merriam Webster Online Dictionary, 2021)*. Different cultures and regions describe intuition in different ways, and while described and talked about differently, intuition remains a common thread of many spiritual practices and beliefs. Buddhism finds intuition to be a faculty of the mind of immediate knowledge, beyond conscious thought. Ancient Greek philosophers studied intuition; Plato describes intuition in *Republic* as the fundamental capacity of human reason to comprehend the true nature of reality (Insley, 2021).

Whether you call it intuition, the soul's GPS, the all-knowing God, or the Universe, we all have intuition, that "gut feeling." We just may not always listen to it. External factors may hinder our ability to listen to it, or if we do hear it, experience can hinder our ability to trust it. To trust your intuition you have to trust yourself. To trust yourself, you have to know yourself. .. and, well, you can probably see where this is going. I think that your intuition is your compass for intention.

Dr. Tererai Trent, author of *The Awakened Woman: Remembering and Reigniting Our Sacred Dreams* and Image Award Winner for Outstanding Literary Work, discusses the compliment of authentic intent and intuition and achieving your dreams: "You open your heart to receive the gifts of the universe and at the same time cultivate your own generosity of spirit so that giving and receiving become a constant exchange." She then ends by saying, "You will naturally adapt your vision to the real world, allowing it be received in the best way possible for all involved" (Trent, 2017).

At first, I felt uncomfortable trusting my intuition. I used to think that my intuition did me a little dirty in my early twenties, so I tried to approach the subject matter of careers, relationships, and friendships from a more pragmatic place, looking at the data. Using my brain and not my heart is how I made most decisions. I often ignored gut, feel, vibes or anything that sounded remotely hippie and went with sensible, calculated, and mathematic. I made sure to comb through all of the data and to not pay too much attention to anything in my heart.

Marie Forleo says in her book *Everything Is Figureoutable* that "your body has an innate wisdom that extends far beyond reason and logic. You can't think your way into accessing your body's intelligence, you have to feel your way in. Your gut, intuition—whatever you want to call it—is far more intelligent than your mind" (Forleo, 2020). When I started living from a place of authentic intention and not out of fear, my world changed. While it may seem like a nebulous concept to some, research shows that intention creates the action steps based on your own intuition (Robinson, 2021).

Manifesting your desires puts joy and love in your path and within your reach. A powerful co-creator, it allows for inspiration, gratitude, and a vision of goodness, and allows for active engagement in the things that your heart desires the most. Intuition works for your highest good to serve you and is deeply rooted in who you genuinely are, your core beliefs, and your values.

UNCUT GEMS
- Clairvoyantly listen to your inner voice and your intuition, and act upon that inner wisdom, courage, and strength.

- Set your intention and all further action in love—not romantic love, but a place of positive energy and unconditionally universal love.
- Intention is the direct action from belief. Every person has a belief system. Ensure that the belief system you have set for yourself is authentic to who you are, strong in your values, and rooted in worthiness and self-love.

CHAPTER 7

JOY

"Nothing makes me happier than to see other people in their purest moments of joy."

—OPRAH WINFREY

"Do what makes you happy" is a common phrase we often hear. We live in a world of happiness seekers. How we seek happiness differs from person to person. Some people find happiness by doing something that moves them toward a goal or achievement they have set their sights on. Others are happy making purchases and collecting worldly treasures or by checking their social media for likes, but these are just temporary fixes. What makes you happy in the moment is not the same as what brings joy. While many people use these two terms interchangeably, they mean two different things.

I never thought much in terms of joy. I wanted to be happy, and I would talk about what would make me happy. I was on a relentless chase to pursue those things. I often tied my happiness to tangible things, events, and milestones, only to be always hunting for the next thing that would bring happiness. The ambitious chase continued. Frustrated, I would ask myself, "When will I know that I am happy? What does the criteria look like?" I could never really answer that question. I started to become afraid that my insatiable appetite for "happiness" would never be quelled. My ambition would give me the world, but no joy.

When your happiness is linked to people, things, events, and milestones, you're putting your happiness always out of reach and attaching it to a tangible uncertainty. Not getting the thing you were chasing is a setup for disappointment. The quest for the social media "likes" has psychological consequences impacting the release of dopamine the brain experiences every time we get a thumbs up or heart. Scientists used to think dopamine was responsible for pleasure in the brain, but we now know that dopamine makes us seek pleasure rather than creating it. In my experience, this feeds the phantoms of unworthiness, keeping them fat and taking up space in your head—rent free (Start Digital, 2017).

"Joy versus happiness" aphorisms are endless. However, here are my favorites:
- Joy is of the soul, happiness is of the heart.
- Joy transcends, happiness reacts.
- Joy is inner feeling, happiness is an outward expression.
- A person pursues happiness, but chooses joy (Compassion in Jesus Name, 2021).

Zach Dean, Health and Wellness Enthusiast as well as Huff Post contributor says that "what leads to joy is different from person to person. Your passions and surrounding communities are great places to explore, and I think the best place to start honing in on a joyful state of mind is to turn inward. I am a huge believer in <u>intuition</u>" (Dean, 2015).

You know that feeling that you get when you are about to free fall into something—the fear, the rush, the excitement, and the butterflies? I call it sick. I basically get sick to my stomach. Some people like this rush. My best friend recently jumped out of an airplane for this rush. She tells me she would do it again. I think that this is the definition of insanity but to be friends with me for over two decades she must be pretty insane.

I distinctly remember that feeling the last week of film school. I was doing what I had always wanted to do—what I dreamed of. I was in Advanced Acting in a conservatory for acting in New York City, and I did not want to leave and go to college for a business degree. I even got a half-tuition scholarship, but this meant that I would still have to take out a student loan on the remaining half.

My parents were not on board with this at all. I had two choices: jump into the deep end and try to make my way in New York City with little to no support, or go home. I was sick over this. I knew I would be leaving my dreams in New York, and I knew that there would be no timeline on when I would return, but my security, my certainty, and my support were back home. I could be who I am—this person who I have freely been in New York—or go home and be who my parents want me to be. This meant being what is safe and defined: the by-the-book college graduate, with a safe degree and a stereotypical experience. Be the poster child for following the path most led. Go back to your box.

When I was a kid, there was no doubt in my mind I would be an actress. I had a creative spark, and for me it was an undeniable fact, my path. I loved the stage, and I loved the attention. I loved playing a little personality, watching and imitating everyone around me, picking up all social ques and context and parroting that back at everyone—and they all got a kick out of it. My connection to acting matured and I discovered a love for the craft of acting, I still do. I feel deeply about and connect with the complexities, the intricacies, and the emotion of the human condition and the beauty of the truth within it. I studied at a conservatory, went to acting competitions, and won awards and scholarships. My highlights, and about as far as my acting career went in terms of being a "working actor" were small gigs on commercials and appearing as an extra on the hit show *Rescue Me*.

When I left New York, I felt that I had given up on my dreams, my purpose, and myself, and I harbored that for a long time. For years, I searched for this other purpose that I thought I was supposed to find, but each one was like trying on a costume, some sort of persona that didn't fit. Years later, I realized that my purpose didn't change just because my job changed.

Even though I never made it big and didn't strike stardom, what I love about acting is still at my core—it's still what I am rooted in. The freeing feeling from vulnerably connecting to characters; the stage, a platform and conduit for change by being open to experiencing someone else's perspective; a place to give life and significance to issues that matter to people; and the honesty, truth, and complexity of expressing the human condition, authentically—that's what I am about.

That's my purpose. That's my purpose and I don't have to be on stage to do that.

When people used to say, "Find your purpose," I rolled my eyes. Purpose felt like an incredibly nebulous concept to me and sounded like "Hippie Hogwash." In my family, your purpose is to make a good, honest living doing what pays the bills. Unless your passion pays the bills, it's a hobby. Our ancestors fought for the privilege to provide for their family. My ancestors migrated to seek a better life—whether it was moving from Puerto Rico or rural Georgia to New York for new opportunity or burning the midnight oil studying for an undergraduate degree as the first person to graduate from college and build a better life for your family. My family's purpose was to put in hard and honest work, not dwell in the New Age pondering of inner purpose.

Was purpose a divine light I would miraculously stumble into? How would I know it if I found it? I now believe that somewhere deep down you have an idea of what your purpose is; your intuition knows your purpose at its core. Developing the sense that life has purpose—and I would argue *acting* is that purpose—and that life is endowed with meaning, direction, and significance cultivates joy in your life (Wert, 2011).

For me, this was a rediscovery of who I am and what values are important to me. My joy was dependent on living through the highest morals of my belief system. I just had to reimagine what that would look like. I no longer needed a huge platform, but I still had a platform. I wouldn't be leading massive amounts of people from a stage, but I was still a leader in my own right and I could still show up here as my authentic self and have an influential impact on the lives that I touch. All of the elements of what I love are still here, they just don't look like I originally imagined them—but that doesn't change the elements or their importance to me.

"What I loved most about acting was the connection to the human experience. To connect to the human experience, you don't have to be an actress: you have to be human. You don't have to express the complexities or vulnerabilities of a character; you can express your own. You don't need a stage for a platform to speak out on human rights or civil rights issues. You can stand up right where you are and do that. Acting didn't make me who I am. Who I am loved acting for all of the things that it meant to me, but I always still loved those things and they could be found other ways and not just on stage or behind the camera. When I let that go, my world changed because I could focus on what I could do right here with the people around me in the space that I am in.

I was leading teams. I made it my mission to create teams where people felt empowered to connect, build a community, and feel comfortable being their authentic self. This process was slow at first, but overtime people started to let their guard down. In turn, they were more efficient, reported feeling good about the work that they were doing, and shared their joy with the teams and within the workplace. If I thought back ten years from this moment, this job is not what I would have expected to be doing or expected to be the career that gave me joy—but that's because my joy was beyond the role.

My joy was in connecting with people, empowering and coaching people, and building a community of trust. The fact that we built cool software was the cherry on top.

I believe that I found joy in remembering what I love, because the things that make us happy are at the core of our real purpose for living. That's why it is my belief that finding joy and finding purpose go hand and hand, and I think the key to finding you purpose is linking to the bigger picture and obtaining a larger vision for your life. This gives your passion a higher meaning and shows you that you are *a part of* and are contributing to what's larger than yourself. I have found that when we operate from the bigger picture, we can find more ways to do more of the work that's important to us, even if it's not "your work."

Thinking back to the pandemic and global lockdown, even in the middle of despair, hardship, pain, and suffering, there were still messages of joy and purpose. The Pittsburg Telegram and Gazette used the slogan "separate but together," in the middle of the pandemic. The headline read, "Separated but together, people worldwide push back against the darkness of the COVID-19 pandemic." All over the world, people reaffirmed their resiliency by displaying acts of kindness, hope, and support for others while isolated from each other. Videos showed quarantined residents encouraging the people of Wuhan China. In Italy people sang and played musical instruments within their quarantined neighborhoods. Across the world, great acts of solidarity and compassion reminded us that the constant state of joy is found from the heart, not the material world (Fuoco, 2020).

For me, it once felt very cliché when people talked about "finding purpose" or "rediscovering purpose." It felt as though they expected a grandiose event. I misunderstood that purpose does not have to be ambitious or lofty to be worthy of the term "joy." My joy came after I stopped connecting the amount of joy I deserved to how much I could achieve or how visible or grandiose my achievements would be. I also learned that there can be no true joy without gratitude.

Dr. Brené Brown says joy is an emotion we all seek but that it's inextricable from gratitude. Throughout the moving interview on Oprah's Super Soul Sunday, she goes on to explain that she believes the most terrifying emotion for people to experience is joy because of the fear that, if we experience joy, it can be taken away from us (OWN, 2013).

"When we lose our tolerance to be vulnerable, joy becomes foreboding."
—BRENÉ BROWN (OWN, 2013)

Brown says that it's not that joyful people are not scared of joy, but that they practice intentional gratitude. She says that we are always chasing the extraordinary, but joy is in being grateful for the small moments. I couldn't agree more.

On my best days I am led by gratitude, an intentional practice that still requires discipline but is forever ingrained in my heart. In 2016, Thanksgiving fell on November 24th. One of my favorite pastimes is cooking for my family, and hosting Thanksgiving goes down as my all-time favorite holiday. This particular year, dinner was amazing. I don't know what it was, but everything was just better. The food was better, the pictures were better, and everyone got along—it was almost a perfect day. Before dinner, we all sat around the table, and as we held hands we went around the table and said what we were thankful for. As a family, we had so much to be grateful for, but mostly we were thankful for each other.

I sat next to my Grandma as she squeezed my hand and expressed her gratitude for her child, her grandchildren, her great-grandchildren, and our time together. I had no idea it would be the last time I would hold her hand. When my grandmother left my home that evening, she went into cardiac arrest on the way home and passed away.

Everything after that was a whirlwind of arrangements, travel, and logistics. Lost in the chaos, I was devastated. I don't think anything in the world could have mentally prepared me for that goodbye, and since then I have unfortunately had to say more than my fair share. In these times, I remember the act of intentional gratitude. Only the act of deep and intentional gratitude for what I did share with those I've loved and being thankful for those moments reminds me to be gracious, intentional, and present in these moments.

I believe true joy can only be achieved when you live your life in connection with your purpose, fulfilling it with the intentional practice of gratitude. I believe that you may have one or the other but cannot have true joy without the presence of both. Finding or rediscovering your purpose can only happen when you live authentically as yourself and have a deep understanding of your morals and belief systems—a deep understanding of what you value. In my experience, I once felt there wasn't anything to be grateful for, but what I've learned is that intentional gratitude is more than being thankful for the extraordinary: it's being thankful for the small moments and the joy in the ordinary moment.

UNCUT GEMS
- Let go of preconceived notions of what living your purpose looks like and focus on the action of living and what that feels like.
- Replace the fear of experiencing joy with the gratitude of the moment.
- The state of joy is the convergence of living with purpose and the act of intentional gratitude.

CHAPTER 8

COURAGE

"I change myself, I change the world."

—GLORIA ANZALDUA

After my "Day Two"—the day when I had a meltdown alongside my toddler—I decided who I would not be but still lived in a place of fear. Knowing who I didn't want to become didn't make the journey any less fearful. When I say "lived in a place of fear," I don't mean that I was outwardly terrified all day long. I lived in a place marred by a fearful uncertainty and a distrust of myself. I am one for accountability, so I took it upon myself to be accountable for the actions that had led me to this breakdown and I was uncertain if I would be able to trust my actions or my instincts again. That may not sound totally rational, and in hindsight it wasn't. There were many things beyond my control that led to the overwhelming feelings I had, but at the time my rationale was that I was a failure, that this was my fault, and that I should be held accountable. My idea of being held accountable is to consequentially not have any further joy because I don't deserve it. In addition to the isolation of insecurity, there was another aspect that was lacking, representation. I didn't examples of people who looked like me, in my situation, beating the odds, I knew they existed, but I didn't know what they looked like.

Theodore Roosevelt said, "Comparison is the thief of joy" (Summerville, 2018). I think that's true, but I also think that a lack of representation makes any comparison almost unbearable. If you are in an environment where nothing is similar to you or your situation, your only comparison is an impossible feat for you. The term *disheartening* would put it lightly. My challenge was to find the courage to accept myself regardless of media, representation at work or anywhere else, and popular opinion. If I was to change my life, I would have to have the same compassion for myself as the compassion I had for others. I had to see the goodness that I saw in others in myself. I needed self-acceptance to lead me to the courage to live authentically and the courage to be truly seen.

The first thing I had to do to make this change was acknowledge, honor, and release the idea of the "strong Black woman." I had to accept that not only did this perfect woman not exist, but she didn't need to. That would be tough to prove. "Even though the phantoms left me alone that day on the floor with my toddler, sometimes their message that I was never enough was so convincing, I had to work vigilantly to invalidate their expressed opinion of me. I could still here them saying in the quiet of the night, "you will never be enough," as if they were the sole judge of what was true. In addition to feeling solely accountable, I was afraid to make any more decisions with my heart because the decisions that I did make from the heart didn't serve me well."

At the time, I was unable to discern that my emotional state was largely due to the suppression of who I was as a person, along with the constant stress of living in an experience that was not only uncertain and unstable, but also highly stigmatized by systems that work to continue oppression. I didn't see that; I thought that the decisions I made from my heart were the sole reason I felt the way I did. I thought I had proven that my heart and my intuition could not be trusted. These sad emotional patterns and pervasive thoughts invalidated my judgment as a person. I constantly asked myself, *If you can't trust yourself, who can you trust?* Because I didn't trust myself, I always felt like I had to prove to myself and everyone else that I was enough, that I was worthy, and that I was able. This led to the pursuit of perfectionism. I had long been a perfectionist, but these experiences amplified that trait and added another one to it: Strong Black Woman Schema.

The Strong Black Woman Schema, also known as "Superwoman Schema" is a psychological conceptual framework based on research conducted with African American women across various age groups and educational backgrounds. This research sought to better understand how to conceptualize stress and the effects of experienced racism and discrimination in African American women. Characteristics of the schema are:
- a perceived obligation to present an image of strength
- a perceived obligation to suppress emotions
- a perceived obligation to resist help or to resist being vulnerable to others
- motivation to succeed despite limited resources
- prioritization of caregiving

Research shows that many Black women report feeling the stress of having to be perceived as strong, capable, and unemotional. In general, for many African Americans and in African American communities, vulnerability is seen as a weakness. This ideology of strong and Black or the strong Black woman can have harmful effects and take a toll on mental health, invalidating our feelings and experiences (Manke, 2019).

In an interview with *Essence* magazine at Essence Wellness House in December 2020, Taraji P. Hensen describes the mental toll of the strong black woman schema: The 'Strong Black Woman' identity suggests that we can bear the weight of the world on our shoulders and not break a sweat. It came as a thing to empower us, but then, as the years go on, we've been ignored because of that very statement. It dehumanized us, our pain; it belittles our tears. We're supposed to be able to watch our brothers, sons and fathers be murdered in the streets. But we can take it because we're 'strong.' We can deal with it. And that's just not true. I have issues with titles like that and 'black girl magic' because we're not fairies. We don't magically rebound from our pain. We hurt and suffer just like others." (Grant, 2020)

I know the pressure to be a strong Black woman all too well. I worked tirelessly on my perfect strong Black woman image. This image was wrapped in everything that I did, dictating how I saw myself, how I thought about myself, and how I perceived what others thought about me. I constantly measured myself against the world and its impossible standards, only to be left unfulfilled, disappointed, and always feeling like I was falling short even though I was constantly trying to stay a step ahead.

For many of us, this schema is a generational wound of the soul, subconsciously passed down as a way to cope with the stress of racism and discrimination. This coping mechanism is another example of the overall mental health issues that exist in African American communities today, where fear of criticism paired with distrust in the medical community creates barriers to physical and mental health treatment options.

In my circle, other Black women felt the effects of the schema along with the perceived shame of mental illness. I distinctly remember the day that I knew there was controversy around mental health discussions among Black Americans. I had heard about it, but I wasn't aware of how widespread the sentiment was. That day, I was in my friend's apartment, and she was having an anxiety attack.

"I can't breathe! I can't breathe!" she said, crying and frantically trying every anxiety-soothing remedy in the book.

"Please let me call 9-1-1," I begged as I grabbed my phone, trying to rationalize the best emergency response for the situation. When I grabbed my phone and went to call for an emergency response, she became irate and grabbed my phone from me.

"What are you, stupid?" she exclaimed. "I'm not going to the emergency room to have them put me on pills where I won't even know my own name, and then have them send me to therapy so I can tell a lady all my problems—Mother would kill me for spreading my business in the street like that!"

I was stunned at her rationalization. Even while panicking, not only did she not trust doctors to help stabilize her breathing—the most basic function of life that we all need—but she also didn't trust that a medical professional would treat her ethically. While stunned, it was a very telling moment. I have never forgotten it.

Shaun J. Fletcher, PhD discusses the Black conversation around mental health in his TEDx Talk, *Reimagining Mental Health Discourse Among African Americans*. In his talk, Dr. Fletcher recalls his discussions with people in predominantly African American communities in the Florida panhandle where he conducted interviews while visiting health care facilities. When asked, people discussed their inherent mistrust of the medical and mental health community. Some people cited that their mistrust in the medical community stemmed from the Tuskegee Syphilis experiment. (Fletcher, 2018)

The Tuskegee Syphilis experiment, originally called the "Tuskegee Study of Untreated Syphilis in the Negro Male" but now referred to as the "USPHS Syphilis Study at Tuskegee," included six hundred Black men—three hundred and ninety-nine with syphilis and two hundred and one without the disease. Researchers told the men they were being treated for "bad blood," which was a term used to describe several ailments, including syphilis, anemia, and fatigue. In exchange, the men received benefits such as medical exams, free meals, and burial insurance.

As a result of the study, a penicillin treatment became widely available. However, instead of treating the men who had the disease with the available medication, those conducting the experiment continued giving the men placebo medication and ignored any other treatments for them in order to track the progression of the disease. The men died, went blind or insane, and experienced other severe health problems due to untreated syphilis (Nix, 2021).

Adding to the realities of physical and mental health treatments is the difficulty of acknowledging psychological difficulties within Black and Brown communities. Admitting to struggling with mental illness is thought to be a personal weakness as opposed to a health condition. As such, many in Black and Latino communities are urged to utilize other coping strategies such as religious community, prayer, and pastoral guidance, as opposed to secular medicine (Vance, 2019).

In addition to the Tuskegee study, there have been other instances that have perpetuated the Black community's distrust of the medical community. There have been accounts of painful experiments and medical procedures without the use of anesthesia, deprioritized funding for predominantly Black diseases, such as Sickle Cell Anemia, and forced sterilization of women of color in detention centers. These incidents, along with systemic barriers to health care and the common sentiments around mental health, all contribute to the attitude that many Black Americans need to have the strong and confident façade (Wallace, 2020). While not being subject to physically intolerable medical experiments, I understood the stigma and, most of the time, felt I had to be strong just prove a point.

I always felt I had to prove my worthiness, to prove that I could when they said that I couldn't, and to prove that I couldn't be broken—but that toughness comes at a cost.

Invalidating your emotions and your pain is invalidating what makes you human. Being robbed of your connection to others and to yourself is an expensive price to pay. A large part of my "authenticity journey" was to let go of the fact that I wasn't always strong or confident. I had to accept that I can't be everything to everyone. Gone was the belief that I am required to meet everyone's standards and everyone else's ideals. I had to have the courage to embrace the strength in vulnerability and the courage to be truly seen.

UNCUT GEMS
- The courage to be your authentic self and be truly seen comes from the acceptance of who you are and embracing the adversity that shaped your character and unique perspective.
- Give yourself the same respect, love, dignity, and humanity that you give to others.
- We may have superpowers, but we are not superhuman.

"Make a choice: Continue living your life feeling muddled in this abyss of self-misunderstanding or you find identity independent of it."
—MEGAN MARKLE (ELLE MAGAZINE, 2016)

EPILOGUE

"It takes courage to be yourself in a world where you are constantly told that who you are isn't enough. Being yourself is the biggest gift you can offer yourself and others. Be brave enough to show the world who you are without an apology."

—ASH ALVES

Twice I have been blessed to lie in a hospital bed and look into the faces of my beautiful babies. Lying there, twirling their hair, listening to their noises, and watching them innocent and wide-eyed filled me with divine love. How could I love someone this much when we've only just met? What do I need to teach them? What do I model? What do they need in order to grow up to be confident, loving, courageous, and genuine women with kind and strong hearts? I can hand down my grandmother's gems to them, along with a few of my own. The best role models lead by example. I knew that for my daughters to love themselves as they are, they had to see me model that behavior. While I am a mother and I always seek to set an example for my girls, it is not lost on me that we are all leaders in our way and in our right, setting an example and leading, guiding and shaping the next generation as they watch and learn from all that we do and the examples that we set.

Know deeply who you are and always be true to yourself. People may always try to put you in a box and define who you are, but you are not definable, nor should you be. What I want for my daughters is the same that I want for all of you. If you let the world define you by your race, religion, gender, socioeconomic status, past experiences, or any other distinguishing factor on which the world has placed some sort of value, you limit your ability to find and authentically be who you are. Knowing who you are is fundamental to doing what is right. Authenticity cultivates connection, bridging gaps and bringing us true, empathetic connection to others. Empathetic connectedness cultivates belonging. We carry with us who we are. Being authentic and sharing our truth allows others to share theirs. Our spirit is a collection of everything that makes us uniquely us.

"All that you need to do, is do the right thing for you and your daughter. As long as you can look yourself in the mirror each day and know that every decision you made was made from the genuine standpoint of doing the right thing—what feels innately right and good to you, how you show up in this situation—that's all that matters. Can you look yourself in the mirror?"

These were the words I gave to someone dear to me during one of the hardest times of her life. My friend was staring at me, in tears. I didn't know what to say, so I sank way down into myself, focused on her words, and found the truest thing that I could bring to the moment to comfort her. I didn't know until months later that she grasped my words and that they would be her solace. She repeated it back to me then: "As our mantra goes, can you look yourself in the mirror?"

Being authentic is not about being blunt or unfiltered but being self-aware and knowing deeply who you are, your values, and what you stand for in this world. Authenticity is about not being victimized by your experiences but owning them and embracing everything that makes you uniquely "you." Bringing all that you are and your compassion allows you to meet others where they are, enabling genuine connectedness. It deepens understanding and broadens perspective. It cultivates diversity and yields the best possible outcomes.

Not all that glitters is gold and there is no glory without guts. My fundamental belief is that your authenticity—being exactly who you are with all that you bring to the table and honoring how you got to that table, whoever's table it may be—is your superpower.

No matter the role you play, from CEO of a Fortune 500 company to stay-at-home mother, be an example and set an example for your children. You are a leader for change. The world today has to be more adaptable for our children and the children of the future to sustain. Those who will lead us in the future must be adapting, growing, and improving on the world in which we live today. While we have made progress, the current state is still riddled with systemic oppression that continues to breed inherent inequalities for people. These inherent inequalities seep into the minds of our babies and our youth, fostering feelings of insecurity, psychological dissonance, and feelings of unsafety and insecurity of identity.

The changing world will require transparency, truth, and the courage to be vulnerable to understand the differences that make up each person. Being authentic allows others to be their authentic true selves as well. This interconnectedness is the inertia we need to move boulders and bridge gaps in understanding: gaps in understanding perspectives and preferences and gaps in our world views and moral beliefs. This work is critical to the catalytic change needed to erase the inequalities for all people and embrace what each individual has to bring to the table. This is a critical movement that is needed in our organizations, communities, and homes.

Being "Black, mixed with," I had the unique opportunity to grow up with many different cultures. This shaped me into someone who sees, values, and embraces diversity. I have the ability to feel at home in many different situations. Being multiracial has made fluidity easy. I embrace diversity and accentuate it. I like to accentuate the fact that I am racially ambiguous. I own it, and normalize seeing people like me, but living in the middle came with a cost.

You must know that the journey will not always be easy. There will be falls, hiccups, hang-ups, and breakups. Equally as important to remember is that while our experiences shape us, they do not define us. In fact, not only are these lessons sometimes the hardest learned, but they are also the stories that inspire and motivate others. Often, these experiences are the ones that nuance our perspective enough to serve the betterment of others and give us the ability to truly connect with others. Through the lens of adversity, we can relate, empathize, and give light and context to others. Through this lens, we can advocate and be a voice for others when they may not have a voice.

Regardless of where you are in your authenticity journey, here are three takeaways you should remember:
- Accept it.
- Embrace it.
- Celebrate it.

Existing in the world as uniquely yourself is powerful. To harness that superpower, you must embrace that which makes you different. Embrace the challenges you have faced and celebrate your resilience and your strength. Replace your shame with vulnerability and the courage to share stories, experiences, and emotional empathy with others who experience challenges as well. Instead of singling people out for their challenges, build a bridge for understanding that adversity is part of the human experience and there is diversity in the adversities we endure. Embrace it all: coming from a place of vulnerability is the most courageous act.

Overflow to the brim with who you are. Let your adversity be the lesson you live by. Your true story may be someone else's survival guide, so don't hide it. Find the courage to embrace your resilience, the power that you relied on to overcome challenges. Live through that each day, not just in who you are, but in all that you are.

Who I am far transcends racial identity or any other marker of identification. I am mixed with empathy, acceptance, forgiveness, hope, courage, clairvoyant intuition, joy, ambition, and self-love—because through everything, the most important lesson I have learned is that I am enough.

What's your mix?

ACKNOWLEDGMENTS

> *"If you want to go fast go alone. If you want to far, go together."*
>
> —AFRICAN PROVERB

Black, Mixed With was created out of the idea that there are many occupants of the "world in between," and that breaking isolation through authentic connection with ourselves, acceptance of all forms of diversity, and embracing our differences and recognizing them as strengths is essential to our humanity. For years I dreamt of this book, the stories that I would tell, and what it could possibly do for others, and for a long time I never thought that it would be anything more than a pipedream or one of my elaborate daydreams. While I curated the idea, its existence was only possible because of the goodness, support, encouragement, and love from so many extraordinary people along the way.

To my husband, Colby: Without your support, encouragement, partnership, and most importantly, love, none of what we do would be possible. I thank you and I love you more with each day. To my daughters, Ava and Lena, you are my world and are so perfect as you are. My hope is you that feel uninhibited to always be exactly who are, perfect and capable of all things as is. The world is a better place because you are uniquely you. Together, the four of us make the greatest team. This would not have been possible without you. The family that we have built is my greatest gift. I love you infinitely.

Thank you to all my parents. I love and appreciate all that you have done and all that you continue to do. I am forever grateful. I carry with me all that you are. A special thank you to Mama Earnie and Aunt Esther for reading through every chapter and offering your advice, guidance, and time in this process. I am forever grateful. And to my dad, affectionately known as "Pops," I truly "gave the ridiculous a chance" with this one. I would never have had the courage if it wasn't for your unwavering belief in me.

To my beautiful grandmother Catherine, my Grandma Cat, who is no longer with us physically but is my angel and my guidance each day: I am grateful for the years that we did have together, and for the unconditional love and support. I am stronger and wiser because of you.

My family, my beautiful mosaic: You have all had a tremendous impact on my life; I would not be who I am today without each and every one of you, those here physically and those here in spirit. I am eternally grateful for you and the bond that we all share.

I also want to thank "My Tribe," the people who I have met personally and professionally who have encouraged me. From my best friends, who I have mentioned throughout my chapters, to the women who I have met throughout my career and in leadership development: Thank you. Your confidence in me has helped me tremendously on this journey. I am forever thankful for your advice, amplification, and allyship.

You can dream of writing a book—the execution of it is a feat all on its own. Thank you to my publisher, New Degree Press, and to the editors who have helped me along the way. Without the support, structure, format, accountability, and encouragement of this program and the dedicated people who run it, *Black, Mixed With* would have never have been a reality. The work that Book Creators Institute does to make publishing more accessible is an amazing contribution to the literary world. Thank you for your encouragement and dedication to supporting authors in this process.

A heartfelt thank you to everyone who helped in this process. To those of you who have listened, contributed, or shared with me your story, insight, love, and occasionally your shoulder to cry on—my appreciation is beyond words.

Lastly, I would like to express my immense gratitude to everyone who pre-ordered this book in support of my dream and journey to authorship:

Amy Sciannameo	Anne Edmondson
Andrew Aimuanwosa	Ann Lewis
Anna Tew	April Aponte
Anne Arsenault	BackerKit

Bethany Forss
Brenda Bishop
Brian Kidder
Brigitte Spencer
Caitlin McCann Wilbon
Carolyn Luond
Cheryl Jelley
Christine Amelie Pinlap Fotso
Cibele Gray
Connie DelRio
Sue Cote
Crystal R. Huggins
Cynthia Hasbrouck
Dajwan Gregory
Dan Boucher
Darlene Thompson
David Calale
David Diotalevi
Dawn Wirth
Debbie Sousa
Deborah Elizabeth Kidder
Debra Ewing-Lonczak
Debra L. Gunnard
Denise Russell
Denielle Greenstein
Diana Ubinas
Donna Neary
Donna Wallace
Doug Bisson
Earnestine Wilbon
Edward Gonzalez
Edwin Miller
Elaine Potter
Elizabeth Bairos
Elizabeth Nicosia
Eric Koester
Eric Thompson
Eric Wilbon
Esther Seawright
Eric Smith
Frazier Tharpe
Gail Bissonnette
Heather Gyles
Jackie Gadsden
Jeanette ONeill
Jennifer Trigiano
Jessica L. Malkin
Jessica Smyser
Joanne Bell
Joy Davis
Jude Monteleone
Juliette Peguero de Hernández
Karen Betit
Kate Meader
Kelly Belizaire
Kerry McCann
Kim Willingham
Laurie A. Cote
Lisa Nicosia
Lloyd Fernandes
Lori Caron
Luanna Faye Arrington
Marcia McElroy
Mark Berthiaume

Maria Panarelli
Mariana Burgos
Marion Chauvin
Marsey Pendexter
Maureen Jones
Mary Ann Kuhnert
Mary Coleman-Harris
Marybeth Flanagan
Matt Alves
Matt Paradise
Meaghan Dunn
Megan Ritter
Melissa Catalfamo
Mia Coleman
Michael Santos
Michelle Dozier
Michelle Hopkins
M. (Powers) Grewal
Patricia Ann Smith
Rebecca D'Onofrio
Richard Hand
Robbye Bishop
Roberta Buratti-Aikey
Rosalind Thornton
Rubie White
Sandra Hebert
Sarah Fournier
Scott Amico
Sharon Cullinane
Sheila Olson
Shirley Armstrong
Stephanie Desmarais
Teresa Loftin
Thomas Olson
Timothy Dillahunt
Tim St. John
Valerie Dupre-Estime
Vicki L. Papa
Wendy Capland
Willard Lee
William Hogan

Thank you all from the bottom of my heart for taking this journey with me. I am humbled and forever grateful.

APPENDIX

INTRODUCTION

Jefferies, Shavar. "Black Men: Stigma, Status and Expectation." *New York Times*, May 9, 2014.
https://www.nytimes.com/roomfordebate/2012/03/12/young-black-and-male-in-america/black-men-stigma-status-and-expectations.

CHAPTER 1

Creamer, John. "Poverty rates for Blacks and Hispanics Reached Historic Lows in 2019. Inequalities Persist Despite Decline for All Major Race and Hispanic Origin Groups." US Census Bureau. September 15,2020.
https://www.census.gov/library/stories/2020/09/poverty-rates-for-blacks-and-hispanics-reached-historic-lows-in-2019.html.

Mayo Clinic. "Chronic Stress Puts Your Health at Risk." Accessed September 23, 2021.
https://www.mayoclinic.org/healthy-lifestyle/stress-management/in-depth/stress/art-20046037.

Meyer, Ilan. "Prejudice, Social Stress and Mental Health in Lesbian, Gay, and Bisexual Populations: Conceptual Issues and Research Evidence. (Sept 2003): 674-697. Psychological Bulletin. Retrieved from Abstract.
https://www.ncbi.nlm.nih.gov/pmc/articles/PMC2072932/.

Statista Research Department. "Number of Black Single Mothers US 1990-2019. Internet & Research." Updated January 20, 2021. Accessed July 12,2021.
https://www.statista.com/statistics/205106/number-of-black-families-with-a-female-householder-in-the-us/.

Turmau, Danielle. "Why Survival Mode Isn't the Best Way to Live." *Psychology Today* (blog), June 30, 2020.
https://www.psychologytoday.com/us/blog/lifting-the-veil-trauma/202006/why-survival-mode-isnt-the-best-way-live.

CHAPTER 2

ACLU. "Looking Back at the Landmark Case, Loving v. Virginia." Accessed September 27, 2021.
https://www.aclu.org/issues/racial-justice/loving.

Ferris State University. "Brown Paper Bag Test—2014—Question of the Month—Jim Crow Museum." Jim Crow Museum of Racist Memorabilia. 2014. Accessed October 6, 2021.
https://www.ferris.edu/HTMLS/news/jimcrow/question/2014/february.htm.

Fiore, Faye. "Multiple Race Choices to Be Allowed on 2000 Census." *LA Times*, October 30, 1997.
https://www.latimes.com/archives/la-xpm-1997-oct-30-mn-48323-story.html.

Mernin, Gabriela. "99 Problems: Shades of Belonging." *New York Daily News*, November 3, 2016.
https://www.nydailynews.com/new-york/education/examining-paper-bag-test-evolved-article-1.2844394.

Merriam Webster Online. s.v. "Mulatto." Accessed October 14, 2021.
https://www.merriam-webster.com/dictionary/mulatto.

NPR Staff. "When You're Mixed Race, Just One Box Is Not Enough." *NPR WNYC*, April 2, 2013.
https://www.npr.org/2013/04/02/175292625/when-youre-mixed-race-just-one-box-is-not-enough.

CHAPTER 3

Donnella, Leah. *"Is Beauty In The Eyes Of The Colonizer."* Code Switch, NPR WNYC, February 6, 2019.
https://www.npr.org/sections/codeswitch/2019/02/06/685506578/is-beauty-in-the-eyes-of-the-colonizer.

Stilson, Jeff dir. *Good Hair.* 2009; Hollywood, CA: HBO Films. Blu-ray Disc, 1080p HD.

CHAPTER 4

Evans, Farrell. "Why Harry Truman Ended Segregation in the US Military in 1948." History Stories. History.com. November 5, 2020.
https://www.history.com/news/harry-truman-executive-order-9981-desegration-military-1948.

Gallo, Carmine. "The Maya Angelou Quote That Will Radically Improve Your Business." Forbes. May 31, 2014.
https://www.forbes.com/sites/carminegallo/2014/05/31/the-maya-angelou-quote-that-will-radically-improve-your-business/?sh=224228d7118b.

Mcauliffe, Terry. "Charlottesville White Nationalist Rally Violence Prompts State of Emergency." *NBC News*, August 12, 2017.
https://www.nbcnews.com/news/us-news/torch-wielding-white-supremacists-march-university-virginia-n792021.

NBC DFW. "Brandt Jean Honored in Plano with Ethical Courage Award for Showing Empathy to Brother's Killer." *Local NBC DFW*, November 27, 2019.
https://www.nbcdfw.com/news/local/brandt-jean-to-be-honored-in-plano-with-ethical-courage-award-for-showing-empathy-to-brothers-killer/2254315/.

Terrence Daniels. "Darkness Cannot Drive Out Darkness, Only Light Can Do That." January 18, 2021. Video, 4:34.
https://www.youtube.com/watch?v=dGooYfMko2s.

CHAPTER 5: HOPE

A Tribe Called Quest. 1991. *The Low End Theory*. Written by Johnathan Davis, Ali Shaheed Muhammad, Trevor Smith, Malik Taylor, James Jackson, Skeff Anselm, Bryan Higgins. Jive Records, compact disc.

Bailey, Chris. *The Productivity Project. Proven Ways to Become More Awesome.* Boston: Little, Brown Book Group, 2016.

De La Soul. "Me Myself and I." Track 1 on *3 Feet High and Rising*. Written by George Clinton, Paul Huston, David Jude Jolicoeur, Vincent Mason, Kelvin Mercer and Philippé Wynne. Tommy Boy Records, 1989, compact disc.

Dweck, Carol S. *Mindset: The New Psychology of Success*. New York: Penguin Random House LLC, 2016.

Hildebran, Gretchen, Vivian Vazquez and Vivian Vasquez Irizarry, dir. *Decade of Fire*. 2018; Warrren, NJ: Passion River Films. Amazon Prime.
https://www.amazon.com/Decade-Fire-Vivian-Vázquez-Irizarry/dp/B089WHGLKZ.

Kendrick Lamar. "Backseat Freestyle." Track 3 on *Good Kid, M.A.A.D. City*. Aftermath/Interscope Records, 2012, compact disc.

Kriss Kross and Jermaine Dupri. 1992. *Totally Krossed Out*. 1991. Jermaine Dupri. Ruffhouse Records/Columbia Records, 1991, compact disc.

Merle, Andrew. "The Power of the Three-Item To-Do List." *Huffpost*, December 6, 2017.
https://www.huffpost.com/entry/the-power-of-the-three-item-to-do-list_b_9512486.

Morrisey, Mary. "The Power of Writing Down your Dreams and Goals." *Huffpost*, September 14,2016.
https://www.huffpost.com/entry/the-power-of-writing-down_b_12002348.

Snyder, C.R. "Rainbows in the Mind." *Psychology Inquiry*. Vol 13, no 4 (2002): 249-275.
https://www.jstor.org/stable/1448867.

The Kennedy Center. "Hip-hop a Culture of Vision and Voice." Hip-Hop Culture. Media & Interactives. Digital Resources Library. https://www.kennedy-center.org/education/resources-for-educators/classroom-resources/media-and-interactives/media/hip-hop/hip-hop-a-culture-of-vision-and-voice/.

The Notorious B.I.G. "Juicy." Track 10 on *Ready to Die*. Bad Boy Records/Arista Records, 1994, compact disc.

TLC. 1992. *Oooooooohhh . . . On the TLC Tip*. LaFace Records, compact disc.

Wheeler, Darby, dir. *Hip-Hop Evolution*. Season 1, episode 1, "The Foundation." Aired September 4, 2016, on Netflix. https://www.netflix.com/title/80141782.

CHAPTER 6: INTENTION

Forleo, Marie. *Everything is Figureoutable*. New York: Penguin Random House, 2020

Insley, Thyrza. "What is Intuition?" *A Divine Universe* (blog), Accessed October 17,2021. https://www.adivineuniverse.com/what-is-intuition/.

Merriam Webster Online. s.v. "Intuition." Accessed October 17, 2021. https://www.merriam-webster.com/dictionary/intuition

Montague, Julie. "Living with Authenticity and Intention." Wholeself Yoga. January 14,2020. https://wholeself.yoga/2020/01/14/living-with-authenticity-intention/.

Robinson, Lynn. "Let Your Intuition Guide You." *Wisdom and Self Growth Department, Aspire Magazine,* Accessed October 17,2021. https://aspiremag.net/let-intuition-guide/.

Stanton, Audrey. "What Is Intentional Living?" *The Good Trade* (blog), accessed on October 22,2021 https://www.thegoodtrade.com/features/what-is-intentional-living.

Thackray, Gill. "Setting Intentions: Connecting with Your Authentic Self." *The Positive Change Guru* (blog), May 24, 2017. https://positivechangeguru.com/whats-your-intention/.

Trent, Dr. Tererai. *The Awakened Woman. A Guide for Remembering and Igniting Your Sacred Dreams*. New York: Simon & Schuster, 2017.

CHAPTER 7: JOY

Compassion in Jesus Name. "Child Sponsorship: What's the Difference Between Joy and Happiness?" Sponsor a Child. Accessed October 15, 2021. https://www.compassion.com/sponsor_a_child/difference-between-joy-and-happiness.htm.

Dean, Zach. "The Difference Between Joy and Happiness." *HuffPost*, December 10,2015. https://www.huffpost.com/entry/the-important-difference-between-joy-and-happiness_b_8771500.

Fuoco, Michael A. "Separated but Together People Worldwide Push Back Against the Darkness of the Covid-19 Pandemic." *Pittsburgh Post-Gazette,* March 29,2020. https://www.post-gazette.com/news/health/2020/03/29/People-worldwide-push-back-against-the-darkness-of-the-COVID-19-pandemic/stories/202003250171.

OWN. "Dr. Brené Brown on Joy: It's Terrifying | SuperSoul Sunday | Oprah Winfrey Network." March 17,2013. Video, 5:58. https://www.youtube.com/watch?v=RKVoBWSPfOw.

Start Digital. "The Psychology of Being 'Liked' on Social Media." *Start it Up, Medium* (blog), November 28,2017. https://medium.com/swlh/likes-on-social-media-87bfff679602.

Wert, Ken. "The Joy of Purpose . . . The Meaning of Life, Part I." Meant to Be Happy. June 2,2011. http://meanttobehappy.com/the-joy-of-purpose-%E2%80%A6-the-meaning-of-life-part-i/.

CHAPTER 8: COURAGE

Elle Magazine. "Meghan Markle: I'm More Than An 'Other'." December 22,2016. https://www.elle.com/uk/life-and-culture/news/a26855/more-than-an-other/.

Fletcher, Shaun. "Reimagining Mental Health Discourse Among African Americans." Filmed September 2018 at TEDxSJSU, San Jose, CA. Video, 19:27. https://www.ted.com/talks/shaun_j_fletcher_phd_reimagining_mental_health_discourse_among_african_americans.

Grant, Jasmine. "Taraji P. Henson on Why The 'Strong Black Woman' Identity Damages Us." *Essence,* December 6, 2020. https://www.essence.com/lifestyle/health-wellness/essence-wellness-house/taraji-p-henson-explains-why-the-strong-black-woman-identity-at-essence-wellness-house/.

Manjoo, Farhad. "Snap Makes a Bet on the Cultural Supremacy of the Camera." *New York Times,* March 8, 2017. https://www.nytimes.com/2017/03/08/technology/snap-makes-a-bet-on-the-cultural-supremacy-of-the-camera.html.

Manke, Kara. "Does being a 'superwoman' protect African American women's health?" *Berkley News,* September 30,2019. https://news.berkeley.edu/2019/09/30/does-being-a-superwoman-protect-african-american-womens-health/.

Newkirk II, Vann R. "A Generation of Bad Blood." *The Atlantic,* June 17, 2016. https://www.theatlantic.com/politics/archive/2016/06/tuskegee-study-medical-distrust-research/487439/.

Nix, Elizabeth. "Tuskegee Experiment: The Infamous Syphilis Study." *History Stories,* updated December 15, 2020. Accessed October 15, 2021. https://www.history.com/news/the-infamous-40-year-tuskegee-study.

Sandoiu, Ana. "We Must Educate Doctors About Black Womens Experience." *Medical News Today,* July 31, 2020. https://www.medicalnewstoday.com/articles/we-must-educate-doctors-about-black-womens-experience-says-expert#1.

Summerville, Amy. "Is Comparison Really the Thief of Joy?" *Psychology Today* (blog), March 21, 2019. https://www.psychologytoday.com/us/blog/multiple-choice/201903/is-comparison-really-the-thief-joy.

Vance, Thomas A. "Addressing Mental Health in the Black Community." *Columbia University Department of Psychiatry,* February 8, 2019. https://www.columbiapsychiatry.org/news/addressing-mental-health-black-community.

Wallace, Alicia A. "Modern Medicine Fueled by Racism." Healthline. October 16, 2020. https://www.healthline.com/health/modern-medicine-fueled-by-racism.